WIDESPREAD PANIC IN THE STREETS OF ATHENS, GEORGIA

MUSIC OF THE AMERICAN SOUTH

WIDESPREAD PANIC

IN THE STREETS OF ATHENS, GEORGIA

GORDON LAMB

THE UNIVERSITY OF GEORGIA PRESS
ATHENS

Published by the University of Georgia Press
Athens, Georgia 30602
www.ugapress.org
© 2018 by J. Gordon Lamb III
All rights reserved
Designed by Erin Kirk New
Set in 10.5/14 Minion Pro
Printed and bound by Thomson-Shore
The paper in this book meets the guidelines for
permanence and durability of the Committee on
Production Guidelines for Book Longevity of the
Council on Library Resources.

Most University of Georgia Press titles are
available from popular e-book vendors.

Printed in the United States of America
18   19   20   21   22   P   5   4   3   2   1

Library of Congress Control Number: 2018932936
ISBN: 9780820354132 (pbk. : alk. paper)
ISBN: 9780820354125 (ebook)

For

Rachel

who was here

&

Jack

the best friend I ever had

CONTENTS

ACKNOWLEDGMENTS

In Memoriam
Michael Houser, Wayne Sawyer, Garrie Vereen,
Ken "Yogi" Bosemer, Phil Walden Sr., Phil Walden Jr.,
Nancy Butts Murray

Eternal thanks to my family, closest friends, and faithful
confidants. In order of appearance: Dottie Williams Lamb,
Johnnie Gordon Lamb Jr., Veronica McWilliams, Michael Brown,
Stephanie Weaver King, Brendan J. LaSalle, Lisa Mathieu Wages,
Mike Turner, Nathan and Kelly Jordan, Sloan Simpson,
and Mary Smith Cousins.

Without Whom . . .
All at the University of Georgia Press
but most especially Jordan Stepp and Lisa Bayer;
Erin Kirk New, Jon Davies, Kip Keller; Larry Acquaviva,
Jared Bailey, John Bell, Dutch Cooper, Richard Dagenhart, Michelle
Gilzenrat Davis, Wingate Downs, Mary Armstrong Dugas,
Oby Dupree, Steve Fleming, Garrett Hatch, Eve Kakassy Hobgood,
Art Jackson, Edie Jackson, Peter Jackson, Thomas Kim,
Shannon Kiss, Sam Lanier, Ellie MacKnight, Kelly McClure,
Pete McCommons, Jeff Montgomery, Gwen O'Looney, Julie Phillips,
Lily Sawyer, Dave Schools, Chip Shirley, Kitty Snyder,
Jean Spratlin, Kevin Sweeny, Bryant Williamson,
Gabe Vodicka

The Fans

Walker Aderhold, Herbie Andrews, Chuck Bertolina,
Ben Bone, Ryan Cook, Amy Dawn, Wesley L. Deaton,
Marina Doneda, Stephen Dubberly, Paul Eason, John Gaither,
Scott Holcomb, Mary Beth Justus, Scott Kegel, Jason Key, Becki Carr
Lee, Joseph Mallonee, Jeff Morris, Maggie Morrow, David Powell,
Lynn Rhodes, Karen L. Smith, Chad Saleska, Summer Self,
Douglas Snyder, William Tonks, Cory Tressler, Hal Turner,
Sumner Waite, Larry Williams

WIDESPREAD PANIC IN THE STREETS OF ATHENS, GEORGIA

LISTEN, PILGRIMS
An Introduction

This is a story.

Specifically, it's a story about Widespread Panic's legendary concert held on the streets of Athens, Georgia, in the spring of 1998. Quick readers and fans of the band will well recognize the importance of the first part of that description. Others will notice there are two starring roles here. Indeed, what you hold is a story about not only an event but also that event's inextricable link to its location. This didn't occur in some faraway rural field, a countryside auto-racing facility, or a municipal auditorium. This happened in right in the midst of the downtown section of a midsize college town that was, at the time, approaching several crossroads. And for more than a few of the public officials involved, this particular event—the prospect of tens of thousands of music fans! in the middle of the street!—wasn't exactly a road they were enthusiastic about crossing.

By the time "Panic in the Streets," the event that celebrated the release of the band's first official live album, *Light Fuse, Get Away*, had happened, Widespread Panic, both as a band and as an organization, was well established and could have easily—almost impossibly easily—sidestepped Athens altogether and done exactly what they wanted elsewhere. The thing was, though, Athens was home. It was more than the place where they cut their teeth; it was where the band was born. There was nowhere else this was going to happen. So what happened when an earnest, heartily determined band went up against a city council that seemed determined to thwart their every effort? Keep reading and find out. It's all here.

No doubt a certain number of readers will want to skip ahead to the parts most familiar to them. For most, that will be the show. And this tendency is totally understandable, since the overwhelming number of fans that I consulted, through direct outreach and from their contacting me, continues to speak of this event as a high point in their personal lives and, to a certainty, in the history of Widespread Panic. If this describes you, well, feel free to do this. If you were there, no one could blame you for skipping to the part you remember best. The saying about not wanting to know how the sausage is made doesn't exactly fit this situation, but there are more than a few people who have no interest in process. On the other hand, you might not care at all about Widespread Panic or whatever this Panic in the Streets business was. But maybe you attended the University of Georgia, perhaps lived in Athens at some point, or are otherwise curious about the minutiae of small-town politics, budgeting, and forecasting. If this is you, I salute you. Why? Because, while I do care about the former, there is no way this book could have been completed to any degree of authenticity without caring about the latter, too.

Let me fill you in on what this book decidedly isn't. It isn't a biography of Widespread Panic, although there is a decent amount of information that might read as such. It also isn't in any way a comprehensive digest of the Athens, Georgia, music scene of the 1990s or earlier. But with regard to this, too, there is a lot of information present in order to provide context and impart meaning.

Overall, this is a story about a thing that happened in a specific time and in a particular place. When I say a "story," it is because this book is an attempt to give an account. I was on the ground that day in April 1998 when this happened. I remember the anticipation, the controversy, the crowds, the weather, the show, and its aftermath. These facts, seen through my eyes, aren't enough, even though everything you read here is in my voice. If the job has been done correctly, you will hear that selfsame voice tell the story of the movers, shakers, dream makers, and heartbreakers that come together to create a singular narrative from varied recollections.

A few notes on the research that went into this book should be mentioned. Initially, I identified and pursued as many primary characters as possible: band members, management, governmental and civic officials. Not everyone participated, but the ones who did were forthright and open and required very little, if any, prodding from me. Then a call was sent out to fans, residents, former students, and others to share their stories with me. More people than I ever imagined participated. Stories and memories poured in; many figure in the story told here. Others, used for background information, helped color certain parts of the story. Still more were invaluable in jogging my own memory about long-forgotten details. It has been twenty years, after all.

The sections of the book dealing with Athens music history are in no way meant to be read as anything other than a substantial, overarching umbrella employed to provide context. Thus far there has been no substantial writing done on the 1990s music scene in Athens, and my discussion of it is limited to those things that I had a personal hand in or direct experience with, but even that aspect was not explored exhaustively.

Another important thing to mention: Athens, a town that I love dearly and with whose people I feel a kinship, is the kind of place where everyone thinks they have something to add to a story. Maybe that is a southern thing. Maybe it is just a human thing. The fact is they don't even if they were there. So I have omitted stories that largely overlap or were remembered so poorly that they could be printed only with a warning that they contained blatantly incorrect information. Also, a lot of information was gathered that would be more appropriate and useful for a full biography of Widespread Panic, but this is not that book. So things that would better serve that purpose and were irrelevant to this story were left out. Further, this book was produced very quickly for a project of this sort, and so, inevitably, some people who might have wanted to participate and might have had something interesting to add have been left out. Thankfully, because we live in a technological dreamscape, there is a way to redress this that would have been nearly futile at the time of Panic in the Streets. If more pertinent information, interesting and important interviews, photographs, and so forth become available, these things will be archived at panic98.com, which was established specifically for this book. Any errata discovered will be addressed there, too.

The call to the public was entirely rewarding. These interactions helped form a solid chunk of the outlining during the initial stages. Most eye-opening wasn't necessarily the breadth of the fan base. Most bands that become huge have a fairly wide-ranging fan base. There is the hardcore set that follows the group's every move, obsesses over set lists and other minutiae; for them, the band's music is an ever-present part of daily life.

The compositional-improvisational rock scene—for a severe lack of a better term, "jam band scene"—is no stranger to these groups of fans and has encouraged, sometime explicitly and at other times tacitly, their development. They are the early adopters, the tape traders, trip makers and trip takers, ticket buyers, and record hounds that are so often necessary in a young band's development. At the other end of the spectrum are the outliers for whom the daily ritual of hardcore fan life either isn't attractive or possible.

With overwhelming consistency and barely fluctuating fervor, Widespread Panic fans, both hardcore and casual, tend to speak excitedly about the band. Perhaps reaching out to them for this book caused me to observe this reaction, but this has also been my experience over more than two decades when speaking with Panic fans.

White-collar professionals, workaday line cooks, magic carpet riders (more than a few), and other kinds of crispy critters—everyone who got in touch with me had one thing in common: all of them were dedicated to Widespread Panic at a nearly religious—even if backslidden—level, and all were quick to talk about what the band meant to them and their lives. Some had only ever caught a couple of shows. Others had hundreds under their belt.

A caveat: in the years since 1998, several principal persons have passed away. They are mentioned in the text, but I did not ask anyone to speak for them. Thus, unless a quotation or some evidence-based source filled me in on these folks' thoughts, ideas, and feelings about Panic in the Streets, they are not included here.

It should also be noted that the people whose voices are heard here are among the most generous human beings I have ever worked with when putting a story together. Through hours of phone conversations, meetings, and e-mail communication, all of them, nearly to a person, was fully available and did their best by this project. That isn't to say that everyone was in agreement on every point. Memory and perspective can be flawed when they try to reillustrate events and amplify myopic understanding. Multiple viewpoints, even those within a general consensus, help create a clearer and more complete picture of things. Perspectives in conflict with the accepted view sharpen the image even more. The easiest thing in the world would have been to pursue this story through only the most resolutely complimentary channels and thereby throw another log onto the eternal flame of Athens-style revisionism. But to wrench a phrase from the Minutemen (San Pedro, California), "Do you want New Wave, or do you want the truth?"

With that, sit back, relax, and settle in.

The story is about to begin.

GOING BACK

As midday descended on Athens, Saturday, April 18, 1998, it was clear to any casual observer, not to mention the faithful, that the town's music scene was astir. Widespread Panic fans were busily taking over every available inch of real estate in the downtown Athens area. As their numbers grew steadily throughout the day into multiple tens of thousands, those Athens residents who hadn't been paying attention to the local press, or Widespread Panic as a band, were either aghast or agog.

After fully two decades of being talked about worldwide—first in hushed, knowing tones among hip, ear-to-the-ground college-radio types, then in blaring reports from every conceivable news outlet to any available ears—Athens's arrival on the music scene had long been taken as an article of faith. On this day, though, as Widespread Panic held the world's largest-ever album-release party, for its first official live album, *Light Fuse, Get Away*, Athens was arriving again. The band—formed officially in 1986, though founding members John Bell and Michael Houser had known each other for several years before then—certainly had. Still, it is entirely fair to grant a measure of leniency to even longtime Athens music-scene participants for being more than a little shocked at the massively enthusiastic reaction from the band's fans for this event. Though the band had cultivated an audience steadily and diligently through years of heavy touring and recording, back in Athens Widespread Panic was always just kind of there as a known local quantity—a popular one, to be sure, but hardly untouchable or evasively pretentious. But just as surely as John Bell never imagined that his weekday gigs in the early 1980s would eventually propel him to the front of a crowd the likes of which Athens had never seen, so too could those populating the town and music scene in the band's earlier years be forgiven for such lack of clairvoyance.

But that's the way things go. Change happens. Through barely perceptible increments or cataclysmic events, its work is unavoidable. Human beings can be curious creatures with a distinct taste for, and discrimination in favor of, the familiar. The cruel rules of this prejudice ensure that most are uniquely unqualified to accurately gauge the overall net effect of change. But that is for the best. We should all stay thankful that no one else can think or feel for us. Most people, when confronted with pangs of nostalgia, experience yearning toward the time when they were either happiest or, possibly more importantly, felt they were able in large measure to direct their own path toward happiness. So it is no real surprise that people romanticize and long for their youth. For those fortunate enough to attend institutions of higher learning, even for a little while, that nostalgia-crafting youth is more often than not grounded in the college years.

For our story, the only institution of this type that matters is the University of Georgia, and the only college town that matters is Athens, Georgia, the Classic City. It is a myth that college kids (and isn't the linguistic shift from "college men and women" to "college kids" an interesting detail?) have always run Athens. But they are an undeniable economic powerhouse, and at least since the 1940s, when the "teenager" began to be recognized as a distinct cultural and economic phenomenon, there has been a push-and-pull between the university, the student body, and the local government. Merchants and entertainers, by contrast, have fully embraced, even made a mad dash toward, every dollar available from this ever-freshening and naturally transient population.

It is rare, though, for a college town to attract a lot of young people that stick around for years, even decades, beyond their time in school. Some never graduate; others take years-long breaks or pursue multiple graduate degrees. Still other young people move to town simply because "it's Athens." The University of Georgia is, of course, steeped in tradition and, in some ways, practically hand-dipped in its own mythology—that isn't at all uncommon for a major university. Much less common, though, is for people to speak of a college town—as a town—with reverence that approaches orthodoxy. Before any musical act put Athens, Georgia, on the map of popular culture, it was, indeed, the University of Georgia that heavily promoted the city as not only a place to be but also a place to long for. A popular bumper sticker for UGA alumni and others throughout the 1970s and 1980s read simply, "I'd Rather Be In Athens." Even the UGA song introduced to incoming classes for over one hundred years is evidence of this phenomenon. The writer of the song, Morton Hodgson (class of 1909), was a wildly successful contributor to university athletics—the first UGA athlete to letter in four sports and, in 1955, a UGA Football Hall of Fame inductee. Still, when Hodgson wrote a song designed to lead his beloved Dawgs to victory, his first inclination wasn't to name-check the team but the town:

> Going back, going back
> Going back to Athens town.
> Going back, going back
> To the best old place around.
> Going back, going back
> To hear that grand old sound
> Of a chapel bell and a Georgia yell,
> Going back to Athens town.[1]

Now, Morton was a native Athenian, so there is some hometown longing in his words. But this song has been carried along through the ages. If Athens is deeply impressed on those who only moved to the Classic City to attend school, it is fair to assume that those who arrived but never left must really be taken with it.

The cultural, political, and legal divide between town and gown dates back centuries, but the University of Georgia is physically located in such a way that these conflicts are often, both fairly and unfairly, intensified. With a main campus located in the middle of downtown Athens, students grabbing quick lunches or shopping for shirts in the early twentieth century rubbed elbows with industrial dry cleaners, lumber merchants, bakers, and children's shoe shop clerks. For most of its life Athens had a traditional downtown with services and shopping fully available for, and quite often advertised directly toward, students but still largely geared toward permanent residents. Since only a squat iron fence separated the campus from town, it's no wonder that the distinction between the university and Athens was blurred to obliteration or that even the most-dyed-in-the-red-and-black sang sweet songs about this plot of land. Be that as it may, most students rarely consider themselves "Athenians" in any meaningful sense of the term, and the majority would certainly never consider themselves townies.

The term "townie," as applied to residents of a college or university town, traditionally means the native population that is completely unaffiliated with the institution. In Athens, however, the term means something different. In other areas it can function as an adversarial slur aimed at the rubes who, by choice or accident, live their lives in a small town that happens to have a big school. The stereotype ensconced in the term is that townies tend to be people who are poorer, less educated, less worldly, and just generally less desirable to be around. An Athens "townie," in the modern Classic City vernacular, isn't necessarily unaffiliated. Rather, it is someone who participates, promotes, hangs on, follows around, or otherwise engages the Athens arts and music scene to a degree such that he or she becomes more identified with that crowd than with the university. Since at least the early 1980s the term has been a silent badge of particular distinction but never one for vocal self-identification. No one ever calls him- or herself a townie, even if such a person has a deep appreciation for not being considered one of those, *ugh!*, students. That noted, even with its traditional meaning twisted into peculiar found-object art, the term can still be one of derision hurled loudly as a slur. Most often it is muttered, judgmentally and exasperatedly, under the breath. The earliest known print appearance of this usage dates to about 1986, which makes it seem likely it was in regular use for at least half a decade earlier. The press often isn't nearly as quick to note trends as it imagines itself to be. To be sure, some homegrown Athenians fit the twisted definition as well, but the term is mainly used to describe those that moved here.

When William Orton "Ort" Carlton, resident sage of Athens, declares that "the B-52s started the music scene as we think of it," in the 1986 film *Athens, GA: Inside/Out*, few members of that film's target audience would disagree. And with regard to the specific scene he means, he isn't incorrect. The B's indeed galvanized the outsider art school and small-town bohemian crowd of Athens in the late 1970s. In multiple, undeniable ways the band unwittingly created a scene that to this day remains beholden not to a specific sound but to an ethos and mythos. Even so, the B's split for New York in 1979 taking its bouncy, Kraftwerkian "beach party in space" vibe with it. The new wave of dedicated art-school bands was edging toward a harder sound anyway. The year after the B-52's left, Pylon's debut album, *Gyrate*, was released. While no one would ever mistake the bulk of the B-52's songs at that time for confessional poetry, Pylon's lyrics often read like an obsessive internal dialogue. Sing along to the B's and you're part of the crowd. With Pylon, you're alone in a crowd. None of which is to say anything bad about or besmirch Pylon, which basically sits at the right hand of any god of Athens music—or, some might even say, with good reason, to the left of such a deity. But things seemed to be changing, and quickly.

Time lines and direct influences are often shaky propositions when members of a concentrated community of creative people are doing things at the same time. The tendency is to credit whichever one achieves "success"—at whatever level of recognition—as the forebear and to label everyone else a follower, at best, or sycophant, at worst. Athens between, say, 1977 and 1982 just didn't work that way. No one wanted to sound like anyone else. To a large extent, the music scene just kind of happened. The Side Effects, featuring the late Jimmy Ellison, by way of example, had a sound that ran down the middle between Pylon and the B's, albeit with a healthy dose of smirk and a little bit of aloof swagger.

If any group could be name-checked as accurately presaging that the "Athens Sound" of the 1980s would roughly coalesce into a Kerouac-tinged Americana of southern gothic jangle pop, it was the Method Actors. Although determinedly wrapped in a virtual art-school smock with eyes and ears toward the UK and Europe, the Method Actors would not fail to make its influence felt on a young band making its debut at a birthday party in April 1980. Co-billed with the Side Effects, the then-unnamed R.E.M. was savvier, more willing to be a working road dog of a band, and just better connected all around than its peers. Mere hours before making its live debut, the unnamed band did an interview on student radio station WUOG with DJ Kurt Wood. Drummer Bill Berry had already been knocking around town and campus as a member of the radio station staff band, the Wuoggerz, for a couple of years. The rest, of course, is history. But no matter which account of the Athens music scene you read, it is only ever going to be partial and, out of necessity, condensed to whatever the tale teller thinks essential. The account you just read is no different. During its filming, there was no shortage of scene infighting over which bands were going to be featured in *Athens, GA: Inside/Out* and no shortage of trash talking afterward. Those outside Athens tended to have a much more generous response to the film, especially if they were already fans of R.E.M. and the like. Still, when Ort described the music scene's square one as being at the feet of the B-52s, there were plenty of people willing to mishear the exactitude of his statement.

Ort was born in Athens, attended Athens High School, and has been known for decades as a walking encyclopedia of all matter of minutiae concerning everything from 45 RPM records to rural postal codes. As a boy in the 1950s and a teen in the 1960s, he was well aware of the drawing power Athens had for touring musicians and homegrown talent. By the time he opened his own record store, Ort's Oldies, in May 1972, his cultural antennae were exceedingly well tuned. At the tender age of twenty-four he was already a living history book on Athens and a personality around town. By the ripe old age of thirty-six, when he was interviewed for the film, he was legendary. In the film, he is clearly describing the modern, new music community, but some folks considered his attribution a huge, encompassing blanket of overstatement. In the spirit of granting a little acquiescence toward their point of view, no matter its origin in mishearing, let's allow they weren't incorrect.

The thing is, though, up until the time producer Bill Cody and director Tony Gayton aimed their lenses at Athens, no one had bothered to set out to create any sort of real documentation of the town's music. Previously, as things happened, any development of the scene was just current news. Thus, no one made a film about Terry "Mad Dog" Melton or Curtis Smith. This pair—Smith an ex-serviceman and student, and Melton an Athens native and former all-state running back at Athens High School—transformed the Athens scene in the late 1960s and caused a seismic event that continues to reverberate. At the time they had no idea, really. They just thought that Athens needed a dedicated place for musicians to perform. One that wasn't a VFW hall, restaurant, hotel lounge, or, despite playing a vital role over the years, fraternity house. Melton was a scene veteran by the mid-1960s. He cut his teeth with regular high school rock-and-roll combo performances at Memorial Park's Canteen. He had been a regular performer at the scrappy rough-and-tumble joint Modell's Tavern, which was way out on the Atlanta highway and, at the time, might as well have been in the middle of nowhere, given how poorly lit and undeveloped it was. With their opening of the Last Resort on January 5, 1967, Athens musicians and, perhaps even more impressively, touring musicians finally had a place to perform where they wouldn't take a back seat to, or provide mere entertainment for, some other event. The cheap but not inconsiderable one-dollar cover charge—minimum wage was $1.40 an hour at the time—was bold and progressive for an untested venture. Crowded regularly with college folks and flower children—not a bad indication of who had bread to spend around town—it had made such a name for itself by 1969 that it was already inspiring parody. Shayne Fair—an acerbic, insightful, and witty pop critic for the student newspaper, the *Red and Black*—held a contest in November of that year for readers to send him a few lines of the most poorly written lyrics they could muster from their imaginations. Fair, who was sick to death of the pabulum being forced on listeners by the machine of the major labels, wanted, strictly for fun, to see who could do worse. As fate would have it, a winning entry came from Willie "Lids" Conrad, of Bogart, Georgia, and his "Ballad of the Last Resort." Dig it:

If you're coming down to Athens, GA
And you wanna know where all the freaks stay
Just ask around and everyone'll retort
That the beautiful folks are at The Last Resort
Everyone's groovy at this funky lil' bar
Every night some cat comes to play his guitar
There's beer a'flowin' and freak-rap galore
And the beautiful people are beggin' for more.[2]

Seventy miles away, down Georgia State Highway 78, the capital city's freak scene was in full swing, but the Last Resort still preceded the deservedly revered midtown Atlanta club 12th Gate by a full year. For scenes to flourish beyond mere backslapping and hand clapping, they need catalysts, patronage, and visionaries. In Athens, the patronage was a following in need of a home base, The Last Resort was the catalyst, and Melton and Smith were the visionaries. But no one knew this then. It was just the times, and everything was current. If any handful of years was uniquely situated for those living at the time to celebrate their own existence by remaining intensely in the moment as it happened, the 1960s were definitely such an era.

And all that is only one part of the story. A gigantic part, to be sure, but still one of many. No one thought to make a documentary about it or to chronicle the contemporary bookings happening on the UGA campus (Badfinger! Emerson, Lake, and Palmer! Bread! Seals & Crofts!), the regular rock-and-roll multiband bashes at the J&J Center out on the Commerce Highway, or the hard-rock phenomenon storming Athens and the campus in 1971: Ravenstone. Conceived as equal parts political party and rock band, Ravenstone was completely inspired by both the Stooges and MC5. Whereas those groups were fit enough to muscle tough stances and inspire people-powered revolution in the quickly collapsing metropolis of Detroit, Michigan, Ravenstone was doing it in a small town in the Deep South. The band, each member a student at the time, declared its own Ravenstone Party (later to be known as the Ravenstone Coalition and then simply as the Coalition Party) as a way to usher nontraditional candidates into the Student Government Association. In 1971 it was a merely a dream, but in 1973 the party's entire executive slate of candidates were elected into student government offices. Singer Michael Simpson was elected senator from the Henry W. Grady College of Journalism and Mass Communication.

Holding that "music is a medium for change," they understood that songs had the power to stick in one's head much longer than dry proselytizing. Conceptualized "during late night rap sessions in altered states of consciousness," the party's ideal meetings, as Simpson put it with youthful enthusiasm, would be characterized by the spirit of "old fashioned democracy where people would get together and split a few rails, get drunk, listen to speeches and have a good time."[3]

Whether any such meetings occurred is a question lost to the ether, but what is crystal clear is that Ravenstone defiantly blew away the traditional gap between talk and action. In between consistently irritating the next-door neighbor of its communal group home on Prince Avenue by flying the U.S. flag (remember: the United States didn't belong to the counterculture back then) and pulling provocative pranks like Simpson boldly wearing a T-shirt bearing the capital letters "SHIT"—which he claimed stood for the Sam Houston Institute of Technology—band members dug in their heels and put up their ideological dukes.[4] While consistently and brazenly opposing an ineffective and elitist student government, they also threw their full weight behind the then-nascent gay rights movement on campus, notably hosting the legendarily outrageous and trailblazing Atlanta female impersonator and drag performance icon Diamond Lil, who first came to notoriety by entertaining sailors at the Port of Savannah. Ravenstone disbanded in 1974.

Many in Ravenstone's circle of friends and supporters went on to have an impact on Athens, both culturally and governmentally. But one person right next to them would connect the dots between the Athens just starting to give a middle finger to the Old South establishment and the Athens that, less than a decade later, would be declared the new music capital of the world. Dubbed the "inexhaustible roadie" by the band for his tireless work ethic and enthusiastic manner, the aforementioned Jimmy Ellison of the Side Effects was in many ways an ideal insider. After working support crew for Ravenstone, he became known to readers of the *Athens Banner-Herald* and the *Red and Black* as critic J. Eddy Ellison, and was for a time the husband of Vanessa Briscoe of Pylon. Even as the Side Effects got progressively busier, Ellison was known to play in multiple bands, notably Group 3 and Mystery House. After more than a decade spent promoting, encouraging, and being a crucial component of the Athens music scene, Ellison passed away in February 1984 at age thirty-two after battling cancer. A year earlier, in January 1983, *People* magazine descended on Athens to find out what was happening there. A now-famous photo of members of several bands standing right in front of the Confederate Memorial on Broad Street serves as a time capsule for those who were there and as an educational starting point for those who weren't. In the accompanying article, Jimmy described the tenacious individuality in which these groups took their pride. "You wouldn't dare play like anybody else here", he said. "You'd hate yourself in the morning."[5]

And it's no one's fault, and no real blame can be laid, but the fact that his name doesn't come up regularly when people speak of the old scene says something in itself. And depending on who is telling the story, there are hundreds of other names, faces, and personalities that played similar parts in the pageant.

Perhaps it is the folly of youth that causes one to think things will always sort of be the same. More than likely, though, it is just plain human error. Behavioral economists call it projection bias, the idea that supremely malleable traits (emotions, thoughts, preferences) will continue unchanged in the future.[6] Thus, the now is held as the norm, and norms are not generally documented at the time, no matter how exciting the present is when experienced. As long as memories are general and open ended, they can be embellished and mythologized and run through our mental machinery until they come out shiny and perfect. It is when one digs down to the meat and bones of people and places that things get murky and hands start becoming dirty. So, outside the efforts of a few art students, some UGA faculty members, and other people of vision, there is precious little documentation of the Athens music scene before the mid-1980s. To be sure, there are plenty of context-free snapshots, a few short art films, hundreds of ragged flyers torn and saved from utility poles, and thousands of rapidly deteriorating memories hemmed in by age and the rose-colored-lens effect. To be entirely fair, though, film was expensive, processing even more, and if you were lucky enough to have access to both video and editing equipment in the 1970s, the chance that you were lugging it around to nightclubs and parties was almost nil. How strange it is to live in the twenty-first century. Everything is documented almost instantly and consigned to rarely seen archives. Untold masses of information are now collected and stored at such a rapid rate that it defies human analysis and meaningful understanding.

The above-told history of Athens music is necessarily condensed and purposefully contains glaring omissions that are known very well to me. They are certain to be pointed out by anyone who happened to breathe the tiniest bit of Classic City air in the years mentioned. There just isn't enough room in this book to cover all that history, no matter how seemingly vital. No amount of historical exposition could tell the entire story, anyway. Not really. Besides, no matter what you read, it is a huge cultural misstep to pretend that, strict facts be damned, a large amount of the Athens music story doesn't rely on myths. Not outright lies or willful misrepresentation but, rather, folklore.

Even though this exploration just concerns Athens, Georgia, and its music, the principle holds for the rest of the South and for the United States as a whole. And as twentieth-century cultural sage Greil Marcus noted many years ago, "It is a sure sign that a culture has reached a dead end when it is no longer intrigued by its myths."

When future founders of Widespread Panic John Bell and Michael Houser met each other around Athens in 1982, the first legendary wave of the modern Athens music scene was already mist in the wind. But just as the population continued to turn over anew each autumn in what could then still be accurately described as a sleepy college town, the music scene likewise continued to create its ongoing story. And in the next tale, these two—and the band they formed with Dave Schools, Todd Nance, and Domingo Steven "Sunny" Ortiz (who joined in 1986)—would figure larger than anyone could have reasonably imagined. Seemingly foreshadowing his future band's willingness to play on low-demand Monday nights, John Bell regularly took those slots at the Last Resort as a solo artist playing troubadour-style. One block up Clayton Street, though, at Abbott's Pizza, Bell was often featured on high-demand Friday and Saturday nights. And just across the street, visible through the huge windows lining the building, was the Georgia Carafe and Draft. It would be resurrected, yet again, a few years later under its historical birth name, the Georgia Theatre, and would then figure enormously in the Widespread Panic story. And just as surely as Melton, Smith, Carlton, Ellison, Ravenstone, and so many others had inadvertently spun whole cloth out of seemingly disengaged strings, so too would Bell, Houser, new proprietors, new establishments, new people, and new places begin to drive their stakes in the ground, throw their water on the roots, and begin to carve their names in the Athens music family tree.

THIS PART OF TOWN

Among Widespread Panic fans there is a particularly fond tendency to regard April 18, 1998, as a day that just sort of happened. Generally speaking, the idea is that the guys in the band were a hard-core set of cool dudes wanting to do something nice for their city. To this end they all got together, grabbed a stage, threw it up at the end of a big street, and held a party for their fans. The first part of this sentiment is undeniably true, but the second part is so painfully inaccurate that it is practically insulting to those that did the heavy lifting. And there was a lot of heavy lifting. Even so, at the very beginning even those well accustomed to dealing with large-scale events and government red tape quite possibly had no real idea of what they were up against. And of course, no one could predict the significant handful of potent curveballs and downright oddities that would be pitched their way.

Although no one interviewed for this book was able to pinpoint exactly how the idea for the show arose, general agreement is that it originated within the tight triumvirate of the band, its management, and its record label. That seems painfully obvious at first blush, but ideas are tricky things, and especially given Widespread Panic's rabidly enthusiastic fan base, it wouldn't be the oddest thing if a random fan or friend had suggested it. Bassist Dave Schools remembered it originating at Capricorn Records. "The way I remember it, and I don't remember whose idea it was, but I want to say it was Capricorn Records' idea," he said. "We knew we were putting out a live record, and we knew that there really hadn't been much of a choice for a place for us to play, since we outgrew the Georgia Theatre. We did a couple of Halloween shows at the [Classic Center] in the big room in

1995, and it just didn't sound good. And [University of Georgia multipurpose sports coliseum] Stegeman sounds terrible. So it seems like something we would have agreed to if we didn't come up with it on our own." Needless to say, the band and label sought similar ends even if each had slightly different initial goals. "It feels like it was a combination of Capricorn Records saying, 'What can we do to push this live record?' and us going, 'What can we do to do something cool in our hometown where we haven't really had a home since the Georgia Theatre and the Uptown [Lounge] days?'"

Longtime booking agent and eventual comanager Buck Williams said, "Well, you know, this is twenty years ago, and I'm not sure whose idea this was. I think it was my idea—but I can't really take credit because I'm not sure—of having the biggest album-release party in history. And we went to Capricorn [with the idea]. But my first recollection of it was just us sitting down with this idea of 'We've got this record coming out. Let's have a release party.'" A veteran of the music industry and well acquainted with the cheesy, pointless shenanigans that labels and bands will go through to push a record, Williams knew this event had to be different. He described the idea this way: "Rather than doing it at some bar and, you know, inviting some radio people and the press people and having little stupid trinkets on the table that nobody wants, let's do this. And that's kind of how it came about."

Now-retired band manager Sam Lanier recalled his first impression by saying, "The idea first came up at a band and staff meeting over at [Widespread Panic management offices] Brown Cat. I'm not sure exactly who came up with the idea of putting on a free show, but it was my responsibility to get the ball rolling."

It was early January 1998 when Sam took the trip to Athens mayor Gwen O'Looney's office. For the occasion of releasing its first official live album, the band wanted to do something special: an outdoor concert on the streets of its hometown. O'Looney, then in her second term as the first mayor elected under the newly unified government that combined the City of Athens with Clarke County itself—a municipality henceforth known as Athens–Clarke County—immediately warmed to the idea. In many ways, she had been hoping for just such a proposal to cross her desk. And she knew exactly where it could happen.

A year earlier, the event now known as AthFest made its debut. Spearheaded by longtime Athens promoter and civic leader Jared Bailey, it was colloquially known as the "Athens Music Festival," although it bore no relation to the two late eighties events with that name held out at the old Athens Fairgrounds. This event, modeled loosely on the South by Southwest music marathon in Austin, Texas, put its first outdoor stage in front of the county courthouse near the east end of Washington Street, approximately a block from the two-year-old Classic Center. Like sxsw, the event—specifically designed to promote Athens music and arts—hosted panels and talks at the new convention center, so its proximity was ideal. This location wouldn't work for what Widespread Panic had in mind, but O'Looney knew what would.

As soon as Lanier made his pitch, O'Looney said, "Let me show you something." From her office at city hall they could exit straight onto the block of East Washington Street where the downtown police station offices sit directly across from the spot where the Uptown Lounge had been a few years earlier before moving into the address next door. The pair walked toward the west end of the street. Even in the brisk January air it wasn't uncomfortable, and the average temperature that month was a barely chilly fifty-five degrees Fahrenheit. After a few minutes of excited conversation they reached the far west end of Washington Street, where it ends at Pulaski Street. It was a broad section of road, and even though traffic ran one-way, it accommodated on-street parking on each side. Right there in front of the 40 Watt Club, looking across the street toward Sunshine Cycles and then across Pulaski toward the front steps of the Sigma Alpha Epsilon fraternity house, O'Looney looked at Lanier and said, "Here. Right here is where this is going to happen."

Since the time of Panic in the Streets the west of Washington has been considered a natural gathering place and go-to event space. The home of AthFest since its second year, it has also been annually closed down for the Hot Corner Festival, a celebration of that block's particular African American history, bearing the nickname given decades ago to the intersection of Washington and Hull Streets. A handful of years earlier, O'Looney was concerned about the monetary waste involved when cities provided venues for Olympic events. In 1996, Atlanta was to host the Summer Olympic Games, and Athens the soccer events. O'Looney was committed to not spending money on things that would be used only for the Olympics, and she insisted that any changes or additions made to the city's facilities or infrastructure would have to provide long-term benefits. "We had made a huge investment in an electrical box there at the bottom [of Washington] so that it could be used for concerts," O'Looney said. Although those recently installed improvements would prove insufficient for Widespread Panic's needs, the meeting was nonetheless productive and ended on a high note.

During the pre-Olympic planning, part of an area known in a later proposal as "Downtown East" was identified as a likely spot for public events. This particular part of that area of land sits just off East Broad Street behind the Athens Banner-Herald News Building. Georgia Tech professor of architecture and urban design Richard Dagenhart recalled, "The pre-Olympic planning, [which was] a volunteer effort, I think, was to have the Olympic venue on the Downtown East property. Pelé was to kick soccer balls around in the middle of the land with kids, etc. And that was to be the place for concerts [and] festivals." Ultimately, though, this area made little immediate sense. It was privately owned by both CSX Transportation and assorted individuals, and it was still environmentally unfriendly. A gas plant that had been on the property for decades left contamination from coal tar and other pollutants.

Dagenhart had met O'Looney when he was running the Mayors Institute on City Design South. Within this organization, he challenged mayors from select cities "to do better, to focus on the quality of what to do." O'Looney picked up this challenge in 1997 when she hired Dagenhart and a group of his Georgia Tech students to design an "urban framework" for the area cornered by the land between the Classic

Center, the Broad River behind it, South Street, and College Avenue. Working basically for no fee, Dagenhart and his students came up with a plan that he was proud of. But the concept was never adopted. Dagenhart said, "The plan was damn good and got raves—but was dismissed by the then city manager and old downtown crowd—and the multimodal [transportation] station and the giant retention pond was built."

In the end, while no significant infrastructure-changing development—nor, to be fair, any infrastructure-challenging activity—occurred either before or immediately after the Olympics, the West Washington Street site had indeed received a little electrical boost. Memories are hazy as to who exactly had the idea for this location as the site of concerts and festivals. O'Looney said it was Dagenhart, but he was a little reluctant to take the credit. "I could very well have suggested [that] location, someplace open and freely useable," he said. "And that location was probably the most logical. I know I would have tried to keep everything downtown." Still, he was careful to identify the person who would have been at the heart of any type of decision making regarding this use: Downtown Development Authority director Art Jackson.

Soon after Lanier and O'Looney had their initial meeting, both met with Jackson, and then the three met with city manager Al Crace. Then Jackson hit the streets, consulting as soon as possible with as many Downtown Development Authority board members as he could. One memorable encounter happened with longtime Athens business owner Anne Shepherd. She and her husband, Billy, had purchased the Chick Piano music store in 1965 after the passing of the store's founder and namesake, Lewis Chick. By the time of the sale, Chick Piano, which opened in 1942, was well known in the community, from its original location on Jackson Street to its late-1940s move to just down the street from the Georgia Theatre on Lumpkin Street. Anne and Billy moved the store a couple of blocks away to the west end of Clayton Street, where it remains today. In 1998, the forty-six-year-old haven for pianos, music lessons, guitars, sheet music, and all variety of musicians' needs was reaching landmark status. Downtown had changed quite a bit in the previous five decades, and Anne took her role on the DDA board seriously. Art Jackson went to her immediately for input.

"One of the first places I went was Chick Piano," he said. "Anne Shepherd usually opposed anything the mayor was for, and opposed any [event that would close] streets. I told her about the offered concert, and to my surprise she was positive." Shepherd told Jackson, "Yes! Those guys buy all their strings and some equipment from us. We ship things to them when they are on tour!" Careful readers of Widespread Panic liner notes will recall seeing Chick Piano receiving multiple credits and thank-you notices over the years. (In an unrelated, but edifying, note Ann Shepherd was awarded the key to the city by Mayor Nancy Denson in 2013.)

Shepherd was an exception among established, older downtown movers and shakers. "Most folks in Athens over fifty did not know who Widespread Panic was," Jackson said. "Several senior county staff had no idea their HQ was downtown or that they were internationally known." If this event were going to happen, it would take a lot more than a handful of enthusiasts cheering it on. Since the show was slated to occur barely three months after this initial proposal, things had to move quickly. For Sam Lanier, it meant even more. He had been managing Widespread Panic since about April 1987, and he helped guide the group's steady but nonstop, growth as a touring powerhouse. The band would be out of town for the entire month just before the Athens show, and he was ready to get things going. And "out of town" is putting it mildly. They would head to New Zealand and Australia—visiting each for the first time—before playing their first European and UK shows, in Hamburg, Amsterdam, and London, and a mind-boggling ten-day run at Paris's Chesterfield Café. Overseas cell phone calls at the time were sketchy and punishingly expensive. And even though Widespread Panic was early to adapt to the increasingly popular Internet and use e-mail as much as possible, connections overseas were unreliable, and even if you could connect, your communication was only as good as the technology employed by the person you were trying to contact. Although the world was moving rapidly in a digital direction, for smaller municipalities and a gigantic swath of the music industry it was still a fax and landline world.

Because Athens is a small town with a big heart and, when excited, a big mouth, word about this possible show leaked out in advance of any public announcement. Of course, even at full speed, government moves more slowly than chatter, and nothing could be announced until the county commissioners voted to approve the budget for community events. It was anticipated that the budget, which, among its provisions, allotted $11,750 of Downtown Development Authority funds to a Widespread Panic concert downtown, would pass. For comparison's sake, the annual Twilight Criterium bike race and exhibition, which began in Athens in 1980, remained budgeted at a relatively paltry $1,000. Total costs for the concert, nearly all of which were to be borne by the band and Capricorn Records, were estimated in the $50,000 range. Because the rumor mill had started to chatter, Jackson sent a fax to both Lanier and O'Looney on Thursday, January 29, half asking, half urging them to have a formal press conference as soon as possible after the commission voted on the budget the following Tuesday.

On February 2—a day before the budget vote—Art Jackson composed a press release that was distributed internally for review in advance of a public press conference and formal announcement on February 4. It clarified the DDA as the coordinating body on behalf of the local government, under the auspices of the Clarke County Community Event Program, created the previous year, and named Jared Bailey as event manager. O'Looney is quoted in the document as saying, "Athens is very proud of its music community and this proves [Widespread Panic] are proud of Athens." The release noted that most of the attendees would arrive from out of town, and it gave notice that the crowd could potentially be as high as twenty thousand. By the date of the show, two and a half years would have passed since the band had played Athens, since its back-to-back nights at the Classic Center's Grand Hall in October 1995. The combined audience for those shows topped out at just about twelve thousand. That figure was almost ten times as large as the audience for any of the band's back-to-back sold-out nights at its immediately previous hometown venue, the Georgia Theatre, where they had last played four years earlier. Keeping in mind the steady growth of the band's audience, twenty thousand felt like a reasonable prediction for a public outdoor show.

The budget was approved on Tuesday, February 3. The next morning at ten a.m., Sam Lanier, Gwen O'Looney, Art Jackson, Dave Schools, Jared Bailey, and others gathered in the commission boardroom at the Athens–Clarke County Courthouse and formally announced that the rumors were true. Widespread Panic would play a free concert in downtown Athens for approximately twenty thousand fans.

Press coverage was immediate, and reactions were generally positive. Speaking with the *Red and Black*, O'Looney said, "There are lots of things that make a city great and convey a positive image. Widespread Panic is one of them." Dave Schools chimed in, "Athens is home for us. It's been a very nurturing place for us, a very artistic community."[1]

Schools said that people should expect an event roughly between the size of the Athens Human Rights Festival and a University of Georgia home football game. The former, founded in 1979 as a memorial event for the victims of the Kent State shootings in 1970, has never needed more space than the half-block it occupies each spring in Athens's College Square. The latter, however, involves a densely populated crowd of tens of thousands of Georgia Bulldog football fans. Schools was incredibly prescient in his thinking, but the most insightful part of his statement may have been unintentional. Because he was speaking with the press in the immediate aftermath of the announcement, he probably gave a rough estimate of crowd size. But the seemingly wildly different audiences for these two events have a lot in common. Falling back on overarching stereotypes and simple definitions, let's just say each has a particular way of viewing the world, distinct ways of socializing and gathering, and undeniably tribe-oriented ways of dressing. Each, though, loves live music and—to put it quite delicately because we are still in the early part of the story—partying. Then again, Schools had seen the band's audience grow for the previous thirteen years as Widespread Panic made its way around every college town and small burg that would let it set up and play. Fraternity parties were as common a source of bread and butter as any straight-ahead rock-and-roll joint. He knew his audience. So he may have known exactly what he was saying.

As noted in the first chapter, it is difficult to recognize the importance of things as they are happening. Unless whatever you're dealing with causes a huge, immediate sea change, the tendency is to appreciate immediacy without context. Years later, armed with hindsight, someone who was involved in an event can still find it a real chore to drill down and attempt to define what happened. As Dave Schools put it while being interviewed for this book, "Memory is a manufacturing place."

Even so, and staying ever mindful of appropriate caveats, one can make a solid case that the occurrence of Panic in the Streets less than two years before the close of the twentieth century foreshadowed important changes in Athens. Besides solidly triggering the end of Widespread Panic's anonymity among the town's older citizens, it ushered in a new way of planning and managing events to be held downtown. Further, though, it would forever alter the relationship between the city's management and its arts scene, opening up new worlds of possibility to each. By 1998, Athens was on the cusp of, and already experiencing, growing pains that were significantly affecting both how the town was viewed from the outside and how it thought of itself. And while its successful passage through this time can't be credited to Widespread Panic alone, there can be no denying that the band and this event it created to celebrate a record's release were as significant in Athens's repositioning itself culturally for the new century as anything that ever came out of a late-night county commission meeting.

As one with plenty of experience in dealing with the old city guard and its bristling, through every incarnation and generation, at newness and change, Richard Dagenhart said of Panic in the Streets, "I can imagine it was done [in a] very much Athens style [of] planning. Meaning a whole lot of talking, arguing, and finally something falls into place because it gathers support from normal people." And he isn't incorrect, as we'll see. Sometimes all that the city ever really needs is a push. But Athens is also well accustomed to pushing back. And this "wonderful gift to the city," as Art Jackson once put it, wasn't as wholly welcome as people tend to remember. But on February 4, 1998—less than three months before the show—it was all smiles in the county commission boardroom, and as word spread through town, the excitement was palpable.

3

BARSTOOLS AND DREAMERS

For most of Athens's modern existence its musicians—and by extension most of what would loosely be called the "new music" community—have taken staunch pride in refusing to copy trends, sound like anyone else, or have anything other than brash individualism direct their tunes. The most ardent holders of this attitude made a habit of twisting themselves into all sorts of contortions simply to deny having a place in any genre or possessing any influences. And the thing is, in bits and bobs, this is absolutely true. But in large measure it totally isn't. By the time R.E.M. was a known quantity, the "Athens Sound" of the 1980s—gloriously melodic jangle pop with a double dose of the Byrds and William Faulkner—had basically been codified in the culture at large and, to some extent begrudgingly, in Athens itself. Sure, scenes develop styles of their own by an organic process, to some extent, and distinct artistic eras can be found in any creative community. But Athens's steadfast refusal to admit that such truths applied to it made it an easy target for hole punching. It is difficult to argue for the patent individuality of a scene's members when one could easily predict what Athens's cool kids would be wearing next season by noting whatever Michael Stipe happened to grab from the Potter's House Thrift Store during a given week. Of course there were notable outliers, and nothing written above is necessarily meant as a rubber stamp of judgment, but it serves to streamline the argument. For all the copycats and train hoppers involved it can be said that for at least during the 1980s, Athens was largely copying only itself. And as one of the leading local music scenes in the nation, that was, one, pretty easy to do and, two, reinforced the idea of stubborn individuality.

At the dawn of the 1990s, though, Athens was slipping into an identity crisis. The pre-Nirvana college-radio breakout of Seattle and other Pacific Northwest scenes, mixed with a large amount of Minneapolis and Chicago—each loosely defined by melody-driven and noise-infused rock that took punk and seventies hard rock as inspiration in equal measure—was beginning to seep into Athens bands' music and looks. By the time *Nevermind* captured the imagination of a generation, initially buoyed by substantial college radio play—UGA student station WUOG 90.5 FM was one of the nation's tastemakers—Athens was sunk teeth-deep into it. There had long been a dedicated group of heavy outsider and experimental rock musicians in Athens, and some—the Bar-B-Q Killers, Mercyland, Porn Orchard, and others— had achieved some notoriety and scored record deals during the late eighties. But good as they were, they weren't exactly representative of the popularized "Athens Sound" (the Bar-B-Q Killers' appearance in *Athens, GA: Inside/Out* notwithstanding), even though that particular sound had been supported largely by myth and expectations.

By 1991 the town was awash with young bands doing their drop-dead best to ape even Seattle's worst. Gone were the Chinese slippers, bolo ties, and granny glasses; in were Dr. Martens boots, oversized cardigan sweaters, and the long-johns-under-shorts look that was perfectly suitable for Washington State's gloomy weather but utterly impractical for Athens's humid hotbox. To be sure, multiple bands came of age during this time that were representative of the irrepressible creativity that was still possible. Jealous as many in town were at the time for not being included on three compilations featuring area bands, it is difficult to argue almost three decades later that the best of these irrepressible folks were in the bands that worked together on *Fuel, ReFuel,* and *The King Must Die.*

Porn Orchard's Curtiss Pernice, whose band had been making distinctive Black Flag-ish heavy rock-and-roll since 1985 and would eventually sign with the Pacific Northwest label CZ Records, minced no words in his liner notes for *Fuel.* Released on Self Rising Records, ostensibly an artist's collective label, it was subtitled simply "Seven bands from Athens, GA." He forcefully bemoaned a live-music scene that no longer attracted audiences from a sizable student population and a nighttime downtown landscape that was slowly but surely being transformed from an old, rundown, small-town paradise into a student-charged binge-drinking playground. "To an out of towner, who's heard all the myth and lore applied to Athens, it may seem that music and the band scene are the center of life in this city. Untrue," he wrote. "Anybody with an eye for activity knows that the real hubbub surrounds the C & S [Citizen's & Southern] bank machine on Lumpkin Street in the heart of downtown. Night after night you can see local students crowding it like prisoners lined up for their own execution. If America has a Mecca this is it."

He wasn't incorrect. Even though the clubs were still booking regular two- and three-band bills most nights of the week, the Athens music scene was largely ignored or treated like an oddity occupied by townies. One possible explanation: the State of Georgia's compliance with the federally mandated national Drinking Age Act of 1984. Seeking to keep secure its portion of federal highway funds, the state raised the drinking age to nineteen in 1984, twenty in 1985, and twenty-one in 1986. For the years between 1972 and 1984, the drinking age had remained steady at eighteen. So for the entire time the modern music scene of Athens was developing, new-to-town college students could explore and enthusiastically support the band scene while remaining awash in booze and brew. As the age limit rose, however, kids trying to catch a solid buzz and a few bands started choosing one or the other. Even though the town was full of lax liquor store clerks, easily manipulated state-issued IDs, and easygoing bartenders, gone were the days of being able to vote and drink on the same day.

Before we go any further, let me make it absolutely clear that in no way—and I mean in absolutely no way—is any of the above meant to imply that Athens slowed its partying or that students were making conscious and wise choices regarding how much of a pounding they would let their liver take before throwing in the weekend's towel. They just had to get a little more creative than before, and most had no problem achieving intoxication. As the drinking age rose, however, student bars began to be concentrated, for the first time, in the four square blocks of downtown Athens; only a few successful ones lay just outside this square. Athens students in the 1970s and early 1980s had a blast cruising Baxter Street, the popular main drag, and the bars directly across the road from the high-rise dormitories of Brumby Hall, Russell Hall, and Creswell Hall enjoyed a brisk business selling foamy keg beer by the cup to any student with a few bucks. The pizzerias and small taverns of the Five Points neighborhood did a brisk business with students as well.

Cultural change was slow to arrive even after the drinking age topped out in 1986, but by the early nineties an entire generation of Athens music fans had grown up in a world where that was the law. So what did they do? A hell of a lot just went underground. House parties in college towns are as common as university marketing materials illustrated with a leaf-strewn quad. They are everywhere. For the new wave of bands, one of the best ways to get a guaranteed booking and a packed house—literally!—was to grab a few kegs via a sympathetic older friend, write a sketchy check for the tap deposit, tell that one person you knew who would tell everyone else, and play in your own living room. While the bands aping the loud sounds of elsewhere were knocking daily on club booker's doors to get a gig, an entirely new set of bands was shaping what would be the next wave of artists to attract national press attention.

Even through this time—roughly 1991–95—a small band of upstart punks and would-be entrepreneurs attempted to make a go of things on the bones of the immediate past. The guys in Uncle Messy took over the empty shell of the Rockfish Palace—where Panic had played fewer than five times between 1987 and 1989 but was a happening spot for all sorts of underappreciated styles (reggae, blues, jazz) in addition to regular rock fare—on Hancock Avenue during the brief time when the building was between official club tenants. Ostensibly rented as a practice space for bands, it was better known as a late-night party spot absurdly dubbed the "Shirley Hemphill Memorial Ballroom," even though the *What's Happening!!* (yes, two exclamation points!!) comedienne was still several years away from passing on. At the risk of sounding dismissive, it was a Generation X thing. You had to be there.

This same crew took over the former location of the Grit, which was at a rundown complex of restaurants and bars known as the Station. Renovated in the 1970s as a modern retail spot for drinks, dining, and entertainment, it was teetering on its final legs in the early 1990s. Although Ted Harty's namesake establishment, T.K. Harty's, had carried on with different owners after his murder in 1977—decades before downtown Athens became the barhopping home of permanent spring break—by the early 1990s it was barely a glimmer of its former self. Harty's was the anchor establishment in the complex, originally a passenger and freight rail station for Southern Railway (in service for that purpose until 1951), and an undeniably popular spot for students and townies alike. But the ensuing decades of all-you-can-drink "Zoo Nights" (a practice eventually made illegal in Athens–Clarke County), matched with the changing face of the Athens nightlife scene and the myriad ways of splitting the student-entertainment dollar, had the situation looking dire. The club's role as a launching pad for a few bands can't be denied, though, since it was more than willing to book the jazz, jam, and singer-songwriter acts that could find little attention in the town's hipper joints. Widespread Panic played a handful of shows there between 1987 and 1989. Even the change of name to the Station and later to Hoyt Street Station, along with its annual multiband "Station Fest" blowouts—which drew crowds of hundreds—weren't enough to re-establish the joint as a clean, well-lighted place.

The Grit took up residence in the station's far northern end and hung on there for a couple of years before moving to its location of almost three decades on Prince Avenue. The same guys that grabbed a cheap, available lease for the old Rockfish scored a cheap lease on the Grit location. They wriggled through a questionable legal loophole in order to sell beer, assuming that they were covered under the alcohol license of Hoyt Street Station; they dubbed the place Hoyt Street North. (The entire Hoyt Street Station freight depot went belly up in 1994. A bid to take over and renovate the property by the Athens Area Council on Aging—which had its offices in the former passenger depot—was rejected. In January 1995, vagrants squatting in the building built a fire for warmth but wound up burning down the entire north end of the building. All of it was demolished.)

Between this spot and the upstart Club Fred—created by pizza entrepreneur Fred Crase in the basement of the Pizza Inn on Baxter Street— any new local band that couldn't grab a gig at least once was either just doing it wrong or was composed of completely unlikable people. Club Fred and Hoyt Street North (and to a lesser extent, owing to its primary status as a restaurant, the burrito joint Frijoleros on Lumpkin Street) were on the same aesthetic page as the house-show scene—plus, the first two could legally serve alcohol. The established clubs in town were run by scene veterans who had their own loyalties to certain acts, but these loyalties were largely to a rapidly aging native population of bands. The bands who broke in all knew somebody who knew somebody. This wasn't a new phenomenon in a town known for its tendency to hype its own insider aesthetic. In a lot of ways, things weren't all that different from what happened in late-1970s Athens. Instead of, or even merely weary of, asking permission, people who wanted things to happen just took up a hammer and saw and made them happen. Need a stage? Scour a construction waste site in the middle of the night and get materials for free! Need a sound system? Have everyone throw in twenty bucks and grab a used four-channel public-address system from a church yard sale. The kids in the seventies were wild, but the ones of the early nineties were coming up from a punk scene that had screamed the do-it-yourself ethic for years. So they did.

To be sure, a solid handful of local bands had no problem drawing substantial audiences. After the 40 Watt club took the plunge and purchased and renovated the Potter's House Thrift Store building, directly behind its West Clayton Street location, it was off to the races. Locals such as Daisy, Five-Eight, Roosevelt, and Hayride could depend on hundreds of fans to show up, drink their weight in Foster's Beer oil cans, and keep the downtown machine running. With this new building came added booking heft, and Athens became even more of a not-to-be-missed tour stop for college radio acts and those just beyond that status. A quick glance through piles of old flyers reads like a who's who of alt-rock.

No spot is more legendary in the Widespread Panic story than the Uptown Lounge. The nightclub opened shop in 1982, taking over the building at 140 East Washington Street that had been occupied by the Paris Adult Theatre, which featured a flashing sign reading "Athens' Finest Adult Entertainment" but was shuttered after two raids and busts for distribution of obscene materials. It was almost as if no one had advised owners Guess What, Inc. that it isn't a good idea to open a constitutionally protected, yet just this side of legal, operation directly across the street from a police station. Thus, the raincoat community's loss was the music scene's gain. But it didn't gain immediately. At the time of its opening, the Uptown Lounge noted that it wouldn't be featuring live music because there wasn't "enough room for a stage."[1] Instead, customers could find their thrills with televisions, video games, and—unbelievably—backgammon. A year later, the club was booking bands. And only a year after that, in April 1984, the original owners sold the joint to Kyle Pilgrim and Duck Anderson. The pair immediately improved the stage situation. As in, they built a stage. No longer would bands set up on the floor against a wall. The Uptown was finished being a bar where bands just happened to perform. It was going to be a club with bands featured front and center.

Widespread Panic first played the Uptown Lounge in June 1985. A mere four months earlier, the trio of John Bell, Michael Houser, and Dave Schools made its debut in the yard of a fan-famous but utterly innocuous, and wildly inconvenient to town, A-frame house on Weymanda Court. There is likely no better testament to the relative calmness of most Athens winters than the fact that this February show happened outside with a keg on the porch. The only photographic evidence of the event shows a crowd of eight people lounging in front of the band, and all are in short-sleeve shirts. Between 1986 and 1989, Widespread Panic made its home at the Uptown and played the club a staggering 104 times before graduating to the Georgia Theatre. These regular Monday-night shows eventually started packing in crowds of three hundred-plus each week. But they didn't begin that way. In fact, Widespread Panic did many a weekend run of two or three shows up the coast or in the immediate tristate region that drew flies.

In 1987, Athens musician and author Larry Acquaviva, a Detroit native, pitched his tent with the Widespread camp, literally. Living inside his campground gear in the backyard of the band's communal home at 320 King Avenue, he was a ready helper for whatever the guys needed. "My first show with them was Halloween 1987. After that, I pitched a tent in their yard immediately," he said. "And I'd go into their house and I'd do laundry, mop the floors, ya dig what I'm sayin'? Wash dishes. And then they were playing Monday nights at the Uptown and doing weekend runs to Alabama, South Carolina, Virginia . . . and I would hitchhike to the shows. I'd try to get there before they would get there, and when they pulled up—and I wasn't talkin' much back then—I'd be like, 'Hey, I'll help ya,' and they'd be like, 'Cool!' So I just started doing anything." These early interactions between the band and Acquaviva are the type of things repeated over and over in the Widespread Panic story. Even in the days when they were each splitting the rent and working day jobs (Dave Schools and Sunny Ortiz worked at the Uptown, Mikey Houser delivered pizza, Todd Nance did construction, and John Bell worked at a landscaping nursery), they always tried to make room for one more.

"When I was hitchhiking to shows, I'd get them all taken care of. I'd help 'em load in, set up, stand there in front of the stage—nobody would be there!—and just rock out with them," Acquaviva explained. "When it was done I'd take care of the green room, whatever the fuck. Help 'em load out. As soon as it was all done and they were ready to go, I'd hit the road. Maybe sleep at someone's house that invited me over, or maybe I'd sleep under an overpass. I didn't give a fuck. Then the next day I'd hitchhike to [the] next show."

At a show during the spring of 1988, Acquaviva was doing his thing and helping sound engineer Bill "Gomer" Jordan roll some cords. Dave Schools approached him and said, "Look, dude, we can't pay you, but we can feed you and give you floor space." Always ready to jump to the next level with this band he loved, Acquaviva said, "Cool! That sounds like a deal to me!" Schools's generosity shouldn't be taken as mere politeness. Although gigging at a rate nearly unthinkable to any other Athens band, Widespread Panic was still very much a developing thing. Acquaviva remembered some weekend shows where "there'd be a bartender, a doorman, and, like, a couple of drunks at the bar just sort of staring at [the band]."

As the 1980s drew to a close, the Uptown Lounge, in fairly rapid succession, stopped hosting bands and then moved into the space next door. The final show at the spot where Widespread Panic had spent many, many nights was on November 18, 1989, and featured the Allgood Music Company. That same night, Panic played a party at the Kappa Alpha fraternity house in Tuscaloosa, Alabama. They had already graduated to the Pilgrim and Anderson–run Georgia Theatre, anyway.

The space that the Uptown moved into was an unremarkable building with an important historical past. Nearly eighty years earlier, it had been the shop of the father of Georgia aviation, Ben Epps. He was still only a teenager when he took his homemade monoplane (crafted from bicycle parts, cotton, wood, and a motorcycle engine and now known to aviation historians as the Epps 1907 Monoplane) out to a local hill by a cow pasture. The moment he felt his wheels lift off the ground, history was made. The flight was brief but significant—about three hundred feet long at an altitude of fifty feet, enough for Epps to drop out of Georgia Tech and open his electrical contracting business, bicycle shop, and Athens's first automobile repair shop, all under one roof at 120 West Washington Street. By the time of his death in 1937, from an aviation accident, he had moved his shop down the street and across from the building now occupied by the 40 Watt Club. While it would take years to happen, Widespread Panic would eventually make its way down the same street and create Athens history, too. But that was still a long time away.

A succession of nightclubs moved into the old Uptown space, including the short-lived but very popular dance club The Colorbox and the rock-and-roll club Chameleon Club, which was no relation to the establishment that Tyrone's once paid tribute to. Best remembered, though, were The Shoebox and its immediate successor, the Atomic Music Hall. The Shoebox was started by Jared Bailey when he was still co-owner of the 40 Watt; it was a good grooming and test area for bands that were either too new for the huge 40 Watt space or who still needed a place to hone their craft. In 1994, former employees of Bailey's took over the space via a lease-wresting instance that no one outside those directly involved ever really got the straight story about. In any case, the Atomic was the first nightclub to begin giving steady bookings to the bands that had been slugging it out at house parties in the new indie pop and psychedelic pop underground. These guys were more likely to be found spending time with their four-track cassette recorders than downing rounds of drinks in a watering hole. Even their band names sounded unlike anything Athens had heard before. It took people a minute to remember the Olivia Tremor Control, Neutral Milk Hotel, and the Elephant 6 Recording Company. But once they did, the hooks were in.

Until the prospect of covering this new scene was simply unavoidable, the local press ignored it for the most part. Even then, most initial coverage was hostile. On the occasion of upstart indie label Kindercore Records' first-anniversary party, *Flagpole* magazine— founded by Jared Bailey in 1987 but by then run by others—was particularly harsh. The paper, still with a stable of writers mostly in tune with the old Athens sound, didn't bother running a story concerning the label's founding or its astounding rate of releasing records. Instead, it ran a release-by-release review of everything the label had done up to that point, ripping every one of them to shreds. Soon enough, though, both Elephant 6 and Kindercore began turning the heads of the national and international music press, and as one might imagine, local publications followed suit. While Widespread Panic had never truly been a victim of harsh local press, it had certainly been ignored for long swaths of time, even after it began releasing records. This may have been an effect of its continual gigging locally throughout the bulk of the eighties and then as a constant crowd-pleaser at the Georgia Theatre. They were always just the hometown boys. Whereas the new bands were inadvertently shaking things up, Widespread Panic was still hesitantly, yet decidedly, welcoming success. The band had never been shy about increasing its audience, and in a lot of ways it was and remains much more welcoming of new people to its scene than some members of the easily bruised underground tended to be.

And while the new natives of the nineties were staking out ground that had already been pretty well trod by Widespread Panic, there was an open highway out there that Widespread Panic was about to hit even harder than before. By the end of the decade, its touring prowess was unquestionable. Up to that point, though, it was anyone's guess who would make it huge out of Athens during the ever-weakening yet still significantly felt wake of R.E.M.'s massive breakout in the previous decade. For most, it would all remain a pipe dream. For Widespread Panic, every day was step closer to seeing it happen.

An aerial view of downtown Athens during the concert.
Courtesy of WingateDowns.com.

Widespread Panic playing for the crowd.
Courtesy of WingateDowns.com.

Street view of Panic in the Streets.
Courtesy of WingateDowns.com.

Todd Nance. Courtesy of WingateDowns.com.

Michael Houser. Courtesy of WingateDowns.com.

Wayne Sawyer descending the stairs behind the stage.
Courtesy of Shannon Kiss.

Moving day with Dave Schools.
Courtesy of Dutch Cooper.

Umbrellas protecting tapers' microphones from the rain.
Courtesy of David Powell.

A drum circle appears. Of course. Courtesy of David Powell.

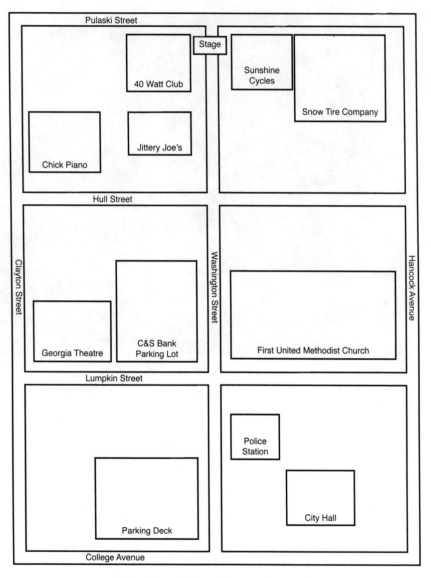

Downtown Athens, Georgia, circa 1998.
Courtesy of Mike Turner/Keyboard Ape.

PROVING GROUND

"Our first manager was Phil Walden Jr.," Dave Schools recalled. "And one night in Nashville, he brought his dad to see us. He was really excited for him to see us play." Phil's dad was legendary label owner, manager, and all-around music-industry giant Phil Walden of Capricorn Records. "After the show was over, he stood up and told us, 'Guys, it's a big country out there.'" The senior Walden's statement was more fatherly advice than critical admonition, but its message was clear: hit the road, play everywhere you can, and become as tight a band as possible.

Widespread Panic knew what he meant. Even back in the pre-Panic days of 1980 and 1981, John Bell was taking gigs on pretty much any stage that would let him play. Mondays, Fridays, any day of the week. Pizza joints, brass-and-fern bars, wherever. The point was to get up there and play. As the decade rolled on, this ethic intensified. Even before the close of the 1980s, the band was playing well over a hundred gigs a year, a figure that would almost triple in short order. In addition to hometown gigs in Athens, which had become multinight engagements as early as 1990, it wasn't unusual for the band to spend two or three nights at venues around the United States. Widespread Panic was becoming a not-to-miss band among a new U.S. scene loosely related through a love of eclectic and improvisational genre-free rock and roll.

The names, now unforgettable, were at the time just a list of groups making their mark via long van rides, a little sleep, a magnificent dose of do-it-yourself gumption, and marathon performances. Phish, the Samples, the Spin Doctors, the Aquarium Rescue Unit, and Widespread Panic joined Blues Traveler on the inaugural H.O.R.D.E.

(Horizons of Rock Developing Everywhere) Festival tour in 1992. The event was conceived by Blues Traveler's John Popper as a Lollapalooza-type touring festival for the new jam-band scene; none of the artists featured had yet released anything like a hit record. Blues Traveler wouldn't break big until 1994 with the release of *four*. Phish had been playing live and releasing records since 1983, and while the band was a solid and dependable live draw, it had not yet garnered the fan base that would eventually follow it around for years. Further, it had released its major label debut, *A Picture of Nectar*, just that year. The Aquarium Rescue Unit was the band of the late Col. Bruce Hampton, who had never attained any traditionally measurable mainstream success. Hampton's decades-long influence as a powerfully creative and innovative musician and composer, though, as well as his preternatural ability to attract supremely talented people into whatever band he happened to lead at the moment, made the inclusion of the Aquarium Rescue Unit here an absolute no-brainer.

The most immediately mainstream of all the bands, the Spin Doctors, wouldn't see its newly released album, *Pocketful of Kryptonite*, sell at gold-record levels until late that summer. The Samples, similarly pop oriented, were selling respectable numbers of albums through independent retailers, but not stopping traffic or anything. And Widespread Panic wouldn't release its first *Billboard*-charting record, *Everyday*, until the next spring. Each band, and some substantially more than others, understood exactly what it meant to hit the road hard and build an audience one person at a time. The title of the Blues Traveler's EP *On Tour Forever*, released in tribute to the late Bill Graham in 1991, summed up this ethos. Panic, the Samples, and Aquarium Rescue Unit rejoined the H.O.R.D.E. Festival in 1993. That year, they took along Allgood, the Athens band formerly known as the Allgood Music Company.

By October 1992, it was time for Larry Acquaviva to stop being on tour forever. During his five years with Widespread Panic, he had gone from jack-of-all-tasks to tour van driver, and the pace was exhausting. "I drove every fuckin' night. I only missed two days of driving, and there were times during [my final years] with them where we were on the road more than 300 days a year. And I was doing all the driving," he said. For the man who had always considered himself an apprentice, the time to graduate came on an occasion that would have made most crew members relax and enjoy the spoils of their labor. "The first tour bus they got, it was at a gig that was at a [place], like, where they play basketball or something. And we're loading out, and Sam walks up to me and says, 'Larry, you'll never have to drive again!' And he's shaking my hand and saying, 'Congratulations!' And I knew right at that moment I was done. I knew right at that moment. Boy, it's still kind of emotional."

As the bus pulled away from Vanderbilt University's Memorial Gymnasium that night in early October 1992, Larry took a seat by himself and got lost in his thoughts. "Later, we're driving through Virginia or some shit, and all the boys are all running up and down the aisle, celebrating and slappin' hands. And then Dave sat down next to me," he said. "I was staring out the window, and Dave said, 'You're gone, aren't you?' And I couldn't even say anything." Through no ill will—indeed, nothing but lots of love on all sides—Acquaviva knew it was time for him, the master apprentice, to graduate. "I kind of made a pact with myself that I wanted to get them to a point where they were taken care of. And also, I felt like I was an apprentice with them. And I felt like they had taught me what I needed to know in order to go do my own thing. I've always been an artist, an actor, a writer . . . and what I was doing was honing my craft," he said. "They taught me. They're great teachers, man."

He made it official when the band returned to Athens to play the first of two back-to-back nights at the Georgia Theatre that month. "Before the beginning of the second show, I got the boys together, and I still wasn't talking much back then, and I said, 'Hey, I wanna talk to you after the gig.' So I got them together after the gig and said, 'Hey, boys, I'm leaving.' And the first thing outta Mikey's mouth was, 'About god-damn time, Aceman!' I mean, they felt what I was feeling," Acquaviva recalled. "So we were all hugging, and it was all 'Congratulations' and 'Good luck.' My entire time with those guys, it was beautiful." For everyone else, the show kept rolling.

As the tours became more plentiful and the shows more numerous, the number of Widespread Panic live recordings grew by the day. Thanks to an enthusiastic community of "tapers"—hard-core fans committed to capturing as many live shows on tape as possible—the live-recording trading community flourished. For all intents and purposes, the show-taping and tape-trading culture of the jam-band scene had its roots in the policies toward taping held by the Grateful Dead. Fans began recording Dead shows surreptitiously as early as the late 1960s, but it didn't take long for taping to become an open-air affair. Although loosely self-regulated by tapers, fans, and trading networks, taping was more or less a tolerated Wild West of sorts within the Grateful Dead camp. Thanks to the supremely portable and readily available supply of cassette tapes, fans who didn't have the technological means or wherewithal to do their own taping were able to relive the concert experience via tape trading. Within this community there was a rule—plainly and loudly spoken, and widely understood to be gospel—that taping and trading was fine with the band as long as no one attempted to profit from the activity. The popularity of the Grateful Dead had soared over the course of decades because of this tacit encouragement, and accommodation via specially reserved "tapers' sections" at shows, and the new jam-band scene of the 1990s benefited from it as well. The new taper scene was blessed with ever-increasing quality from the rapidly evolving technology of the day, and there is something undeniably special about being able to relive, through a decent audio recording, a great experience at a show. In the twenty-first century, when anything can be recorded by one's telephone, it is a difficult bit of musical history to impart to casual fans.

With the rise of the early-1990s jam-band scene—a contentious term used here for convenience's sake—as natural heir to the legacy of the Grateful Dead, it's no surprise that the tape culture bled over, too. Further, the Dead experienced the height of its pop culture fever in the late 1980s, gaining many first-time listeners. As a certain amount of these fans went deeper into the scene and became interested in taping, it seems pretty natural that they would be interested in finding a band of their own, so to speak. One they could be on the ground floor with.

And Widespread Panic, Phish, and a few others were ripe young acts with nonstop touring schedules, lots of material and varied set lists, and a similarly relaxed attitude toward fans recording live shows. The release of official live albums by rock artists reached a peak in the 1970s, and for a lot of fans they provided a first entrée into a group's music. The Allman Brothers broke out in a big way courtesy of their raw barnburner double LP from 1971, *At Fillmore East*. That same year, the English blues-rock band Humble Pie released *Performance Rockin' the Fillmore*. Five years later, Humble Pie guitarist Peter Frampton released the chart-topping, but convenient argument starter, *Frampton Comes Alive*. Although all the basic tracks were indeed recorded live, there was just enough studio surgery to lead to decades of arguing over whether *Frampton Comes Alive* truly constituted a "live" record. After all, most bands recorded live as a group in the studio, so what was the difference if tracks recorded onstage were going to be over-dubbed in the studio later? The Grateful Dead's gold-selling (and eventual double-platinum-selling) live triple LP *Europe '72* underwent similar studio manipulation.

S. Alexander Reed, an assistant professor of music theory at the University of Florida, in a 2005 paper presented at the Art of Record Production conference at the University of Westminster noted, "Not only is the division between live performance and studio production confounded by the mere existence of concert recordings, but it is deeply blurred in practice by the highly studio-centric process of engineering, mixing, remixing, and otherwise producing a contemporary live record. It is not uncommon for performers' mistakes to be edited, pitch-corrected, or overdubbed entirely, nor is it atypical for an engineer to alter equalization, phasing, or reverberation to account for discrepancies between the desired acoustics of the recording and those of the concert venue."[1] This is precisely what occurred with both Frampton and the Dead on the above-referenced records.

Some rock-and-roll audiences have been obsessed with an authenticity that, while ostensibly admirable, may be unobtainable and may, indeed, represent a false dichotomy between the real and unreal. Reed said in the same presentation, "Legend is a good way to think about live records, because our understanding of legendary events concedes that maybe they didn't really happen the way we tell it, and maybe they never happened at all, and maybe their characters never even existed, *but that makes them no less true.* Stories come from culture, but cultures come from legends. In this respect, the realm of Legend gives us perhaps the original hyperreal simulacrum . . . And so the truth of a recording is more important than the reality of a recording" (emphasis in the original).[2]

The quest for authenticity in the tape-trading community can be characterized by the quest for a sound as close to an original source as possible. A nondegraded, high-quality source recording is paramount, and traders have long been keen to know exactly what they are getting.

Before the rise of digital downloading and an infinitely searchable database of recordings came into being, a fan typically joined the taping community by being turned on to, or given outright, some tapes by a friend or fellow fan. Then, once taken in, fans would scour classified ads and want lists placed by other traders in the back of magazines like the Grateful Dead fan publication *Relix* or the record-collector magazine *Goldmine*. A typical ad might read: "Trader in Georgia with GD/JGB [Grateful Dead/Jerry Garcia band] seeks more, HQ [high quality] only, your list gets mine." Money wasn't part of the exchange, so once an agreement to swap shows was agreed upon, each trader would make copies for the other party. If one side of the exchange didn't have any desirable material for the other, the tape requester would commonly send "b & p" (blank tapes and postage) to the person doing the dubbing. There weren't many Widespread Panic recordings available at the start of the 1990s, although as one fan reported, "In the scheme of things nationally, their fan base was a blip in the Grateful Dead scene." This all changed with the launch of Spreadnet.

Spreadnet, the original online listserv for Widespread Panic fans, was launched via Brown University's Netspace project in 1994. The service allowed fans to pass along gossip and news, get in touch electronically, and, most importantly, source Widespread Panic live recordings directly from one another. No longer were they at the mercy of limited ad space in monthly publications, nor did they have to settle for collections of afterthoughts from fans more committed to other artists.

If there was a particularly good recording of a show or if someone had captured a show that was unusually desirable because of the performance, someone in the community would organize a "tree." This tape tree was "seeded" by an original high-quality recording—usually created with portable Digital Audio Tape recorders—and organized as a series of leafs and branches. Fans that signed on to be a leaf would get a cassette copy of the show. Those who volunteered to be branches would generally receive a high-quality DAT copy and agree to make first-generation cassette copies for leaves on their branch. For a show expected to be a hot item, the tree would be organized in advance. The modern jam-band torrent site etree.com takes its name from this process. But in the old days of Spreadnet, only the tree itself was organized electronically via the Internet. Tapes were still duplicated in real time and sent through the mail. No one was transmitting digital files at the time. Although the MP3 coding format was released circa 1993, no audiophile considered this lossy format "high quality," and in any case, no one was swapping digital files in any sizable quantity until the end of the decade. Only with the expansive spread of high-speed Internet access a few year later were fans swapping extremely high-quality loss-less files online.

Another way that tapes got passed around was by fans coordinating taping get-togethers. A group of tapers in a city, each likely armed with a DAT machine, would organize a potluck dinner or similar kind of gathering at a house. Attendees would show up with their DAT or cassette decks and blank tapes. A consensus would be arrived at concerning which original recording of the same recent show was the best or most wanted, and then the dubbing would begin. The best original would serve as the source material for everyone. Everyone would leave with a copy of the show. Those lucky enough to own one of the early-generation stand-alone CD burners would take home an artifact that the common person could only dream of possessing, since compact disc technology had always been tightly controlled and prohibitively expensive.

"We frustrated and boggled every label we ever had, because they could see the kind of crowds we could draw and they'd try to do some sort of tricky record company math and say, 'We can sell a record to every one of these people,'" said Dave Schools. "The record company loves to blame the taping community for the lack of sales of records. But those tapers are fanatics. They've already bought the studio records. They want more. This is something that labels have never understood, and may be one of the reasons that streaming is so popular and why labels deteriorated so quickly."

Indeed, Widespread Panic had established a pretty clear policy with regard to taping by 1995. It was stated in their newsletter *Moon Times*: "We realize that the Panic experience is something many of you wish to remember long after the show is over. In the interest of making things easier for all of us, here are a few ground rules. First, Panic allows the taping of shows for personal use only. Please feel free to trade but never sell a tape! Second, audience tapes are all we allow so please come with your own mics and power supply! Our crew is too busy dealing with the hassles of putting on the show to help you locate building power. Third, some venues adhere to strict union rules and this often includes a 'no audio recording' clause. In these cases we try to get the union to lighten up but sometimes it just doesn't work. These are the cases in which you'll be left to your own devices to get your gear in the building (remember the days before there was a taping section and it was fun to sneak your gear in?). Fourth, remember that there are other people who came to see the show and may not want to deal with mics ten feet in the air right in front of them so please try to be considerate when choosing a location from which to tape. Lastly, have fun! Documentation is important so let the tapes roll!"

The accessibility of the consumer-grade CD burner, though, opened a floodgate of issues. It ensured that anything burned to this digital medium would be a perfect match sonically to whatever source was used, and the process could be repeated infinitely. A copy of a CD would always be as good as the original CD. Selling copies of shows had always been a forbidden activity, even for bands with generous taping policies. While research for this book turned up no reports of traditional tape traders participating in the CD-for-profit game once high-quality CD copies started traversing the globe, there was no stopping nefarious characters from doing just that. A legal loophole in several European nations held that live recordings or unreleased material didn't qualify for copyright protection, as legitimately released albums did, so bootleggers employed pressing plants in Italy and France to manufacture their wares. It is suspected, too, that pressing plants and duplication facilities in the United States and Canada were used for this purpose, but were stamped "Made in Italy" to avoid detection. Thus, these recordings became euphemistically referred to as "imports" in record-store lingo. Customers walking into retail record shops, which were nearly always independent, mom-and-pop shops, and asking for "imports" were, rest assured, not looking for a 12" UK dance remix. They wanted the live goods.

The local record stores in Athens were all too eager to meet customer demand. In retrospect, the process was a laughably cloak-and-dagger operation. Once every week or two, bootleg wholesalers would send out a fax with their current offerings. There was never a return number on the fax. Record stores that had proved reliable—meaning they had bought product and wouldn't rat out the wholesalers to the RIAA (Record Industry Association of America) or law enforcement—would be given a phone number to call with their order. Then, like clockwork, someone would arrive within a few days with a plastic tub or cardboard box full of shiny packages. Payment was settled with cash or a company check for "used CDs." Through this process, an entirely new generation of fans, who were completely unaware that tape trading existed as a sharing community, wound up spending untold sums of money because they thought the material could be had only this way. Stores in Athens did a brisk business of selling single, double, and triple CD sets for $26, $52, and $65 each. The doubles were the most common; jam bands typically played two sets lasting at least an hour each during a show. But if a customer wanted, say, a special New Year's Eve show by Widespread Panic or an envied all-covers Halloween tribute set by Phish, they had to lay out serious cash. Those involved in the tape-trading community, as general rule, weren't having any of this. "[The] trading of tapes [was] self-monitored by the traders," Buck Williams said. "When people started bootlegging and selling shows, the traders wouldn't have it. They'd boycott. They knew it was wrong, and they'd boycott it."

The bands in the scene understood why someone would buy the bootleg CDs, though. Although they would never approve of shady characters charging ridiculous prices for these packages, they were all old-school record-store hounds and rock fans. They understood how excited a hard-core fan could get at the possibility of hearing something from their favorite band that wasn't on one of the official releases, all of which they had undoubtedly already purchased. Still, the prospect of having a beautifully mastered, handpicked set of live material released in a nice package was a hallmark type of release for bands of this era, which had grown up on such meaty albums as *At Fillmore East* and Little Feat's *Waiting for Columbus*. Widespread Panic had been on a years-long creative trajectory of five studio albums—in a mere eight and a half years—in addition to a nonstop touring regimen. As the nineties really heated up, fans got a triple threat of powerful records: their Capricorn Records debut *Ain't Life Grand*, the grand and dark *Everyday*, and *Bombs & Butterflies*, which included stellar versions of Pops Staples's "Hope in a Hopeless World" and Vic Chesnutt's "Aunt Avis." So even though there was an untold wealth of live material available for Widespread Panic's fans to hear through both community and criminal means, it was time for the band to re-lease its own live album.

For an official live album, the band would have the upper hand in its recording, packaging, and overall presentation. Williams said, "It was part of [the band's record] deal, and so many record deals, particularly at that time, included a live record. It was a way of getting another record out without having to pay studio costs and this, that, and the other. So it was standard. Widespread Panic wasn't big on sell-ing records, but they were selling a quarter of a million, three hundred thousand of each one, which was very decent. [*Light Fuse, Get Away* was] an official product, and the difference was we had [professional] masters, we had studio mixes. This wasn't like what you were getting from the taper's stand. It was a whole different level musically. We thought it was time."

For many bands, the contractually obligated live album—a standard line item for a lot of bands working with traditional record contracts—is a half-hearted, bogus affair that the band does as a stand-in for a studio album, and the fans don't care about it. "In 99 out of 100 cases of a live album, it's a contract filler demanded as something extra out of the band by the label," said Schools. "And often, if the band is in a creative dip, that's a stopgap. You know, 'Let's crank out a live record.' And they're usually poor quality. [But] for bands like the Dead and Allman Brothers and Little Feat, you have to look at these monumentally valuable live records. Allman Brothers didn't sell shit of their first two records they did in a studio. Then they put out the famous *At Fillmore East* record, and shit blew up because people were given a high-quality product that represented the band well."

LAWYERS, GUNS, AND MONEY

On March 17, 1998, a line out of left field was drawn in the sand. "They say you can't fight City Hall. Well, by gosh, I can," Carroll "Oby" Dupree was reported as saying by the press following the developing story of the as-yet-unnamed event slated to take place the next month.[1] The longtime Athens resident had spent the previous year planning her daughter's wedding, and it was slated to take place at the First United Methodist Church at the corner of Lumpkin and Washington on April 18. Dupree had become aware of Widespread Panic's plans only in early March, and by midmonth, barely four weeks until show time, Dupree and the city were at an impasse. The Athens Downtown Development Authority was sympathetic to her problem and offered concessions as issues were presented, but remained steadfast in wanting to go ahead with the show. The press reported that Dupree warned she had already been in touch with a couple of lawyers and would do anything in her power to have the show moved. Art Jackson had suggested that the wedding guests be given exclusive parking downtown and perhaps even some sort of shuttle service. He suggested the band rethink the starting time in order to give the happy couple a chance to exchange vows in peace.

Dupree's stress was certainly understandable. Her daughter, Mary Carroll Dillard, was expecting upward of seven hundred guests, and no small amount of preparation had already taken place. Dupree, who wasn't one to give in easily, stood her ground, even though she seemed to recognize Jackson's efforts. She is reported, but not confirmed, as having said, "Mr. Jackson certainly seems to care. But I won't settle for anything less than them moving the concert. This is my daughter's dream, and I want to see that she has it."

Gwen O'Looney, in an update sent out to the county commission and city manager a few days later, remarked, "The bride's mother has not been willing to define what is needed to accommodate the two events [the wedding and the concert] other than her desire that the event be moved or cancelled." Quite correctly, O'Looney noted that it would be bad precedent to allow a scheduled private event to dictate the activities of the city at large and the DDA in particular."

Although there were definite, tangible concerns on Dupree's part, the press—especially the small-town local press, which loves a good down-home conflict story—seemed to take one or two memorable comments and spin solid gold barbed wire out of them. "It really was a funny situation," Dupree said. "But I have to tell you, the media—and I don't just mean the local media … If you pull up my name, you can pull up [even] from other states all this stuff. And it was so not true. I mean, the media reported all this stuff. Supposedly, I had all these conversations that never took place. They would say things like, 'Mom of the bride still not happy,' and I'd turn to my friends and say, 'What are they talking about? I don't even know what they're talking about.'" Dupree remembered the entire kerfuffle with a distinct eye and ear for bullshit but also with a southern firecracker's sense of humor, wit, and charm. Even she, though, recalled clearly the stress of the situation and the need for immediate action. "Once we found out [about the concert], of course we just about had a heart attack," she said. "And my daughter just had too much on her mind to even deal with it. And what are mothers for? It just was one of those things where I, I guess you could say, felt panicked at first. I had widespread panic! And that's the truth! I really did."

In some ways, Dupree's concerns echoed those already swirling round the concert organizers. After the initial rush of excitement had faded, the tut-tutting and handwringing began. Almost immediately there were concerns regarding potentially enormous costs for city services: police and fire, but also solid waste, portable toilets, and parking. Even though Athens was well acclimated to hosting outrageously enthusiastic Georgia Bulldog football fans several weekends a year, that was a devil Athens knew. Where it was headed now was uncharted territory.

In Athens, anyone receiving a service from the city is on the hook for paying for it, and that's entirely reasonable. On the flip side, it's also reasonable to let people know how much a service is going to cost. During the course of planning the show, the goalposts kept moving. The largest ongoing downtown event at the time was the Twilight Criterium, which was the scene of drunken hordes and ramblin' wrecks until the city tightened up its alcohol permissions, and Gwen O'Looney was of the opinion that Widespread Panic should be given the same consideration. "I had a manager then named Al Crace . . . [and] he fought me every inch of the way on this," she said. "He was my favorite manager, and he and I were partners in so much. There is a clause in our charter that says that anyone that receives a service must pay for the service. And so he really was very hard on [Widespread Panic]. I didn't mind him charging what he charged Twilight and other things that were happening, but he kept pulling up new things. I'd say, 'Look, set your bill and stop changing it. It's not fair.'"

This kind of frustration wouldn't have been an issue a decade earlier. Before the unification of the City of Athens and Clarke County, Athens had enjoyed what is known as a "strong mayor–council" system. That is, the buck stopped with the mayor. While there remained a distinct legislative divide between the mayor and his or her city council, the mayor was the chief executive in charge of city business. Under this system, the mayor served as the chief executive officer—during O'Looney's first mayoral run, she was elected "CEO," but that meant chief elected officer—and could hire and fire department heads, create and enforce the city budget, and more. The city council was charged with creating city policies via ordinances.[2] Under the newly adopted "weak mayor–council" system—the acceptance of which was the only way Clarke County was ever going to agree to unification, since the county feared being under the ruling authority of a strong Athens mayor—the mayor's role was primarily window dressing.[3] Weak mayors have nearly none of the power wielded by strong mayors. Thus, Gwen O'Looney was not only the first progressive female mayor of Athens—and fit to endure all the good-old-boy blowback that engendered—but also the first mayor whose duties were reduced to being able to determine agenda items for meetings of the county commission, presenting the city budget, and merely having the ability to make recommendations for who to hire as city manager, attorney, judge of the municipal court, and internal city auditor. For the eternally energetic, engaged, and enthusiastic O'Looney, this must have seemed, at times, something like an inverted Leibnizian universe comprising the worst of all possible worlds.

Even so, a group of people working together, every single day at a minimum and around the clock on some days, dug in and started getting their hands dirty. Jackson, Lanier, and Bailey held a meeting on February 17 with representatives from Alcohol Beverage Control, the director of downtown parking services, representatives from the police, fire and sheriff's departments, Jeff Montgomery from the Public Information Office, and Angel Helmly from Central Services. Though the minutes of the meeting reveal a productive discussion, a telling notation indicates that the consensus was "great for community and business, a royal pain in the neck for Fire, Police, and Sherriff's Department." In part, the uniqueness of the concert was a concern: "Unlike UGA football crowds, people won't know where to go and will be concentrated downtown. If this event isn't going to happen [it] has to be decided ASAP. Although it seems like everyone will grudgingly work together."

Preliminary plans with regard to rolling street closures had been created the week before, and they indicated that the block directly in front of the stage would close at three a.m. the day of the show, the next block—between Hull and Lumpkin—at two p.m., and the final stretch, between Lumpkin and College Avenue, at six p.m. The far-back parking behind the First United Methodist Church, a stretch of land that included an old Athens police filling station, was established as a vendor area for food and beverages. Sound relay towers would be placed at three-hundred-foot intervals for the three blocks east of Washington past Hull. Port-a-johns would be located in both this area and two blocks away at the corner of Washington and College. And even though improvements to the electrical capacity of the staging area had been made a couple of years earlier, the power was still insufficient for the show Widespread Panic had planned. Figures started being thrown around about the cost of additional improvements, expenses that would land squarely on the shoulders of the band. Overall, things were coming together, even though the discussions were tense and some participants trepidatious. And though negotiations had begun in February, it wasn't until March 5 that Art Jackson completed the formal application for the event.

The first department to respond with a cost estimate was the Athens–Clarke County Police. Ninety-seven police personnel were expected to work an estimated 1,054 hours of overtime at a cost of $44,455. This was in addition to the regular-time estimate of $35,890 for the area known as the Central Business District (CBD) of downtown. This estimate would hold if and only if the CBD did not reach a point of "gridlock," although on police department records dated March 27, 1998, a handwritten notation states, "The Georgia State Patrol believes [gridlock is] a near certainty. If grid lock occurs the cost will increase above [this figure]."

Twenty miles outside town, in Commerce, Georgia, the Atlanta International Speedway had scheduled a weekend of drag races for April 17–19, and Athens was the closest place for those attendees to book hotel rooms. And sure enough, they had. And the police department notes indicate that the department was fearful that "90,000–100,000 race fans" would make their way down from Commerce to attend this "non-ticketed event," but admitted, "How can we know?" While the chances of one hundred thousand car-racing fans driving down the two-lane 441 South to just randomly show up for this street party, all in the middle of their already-paid-for race weekend, was slim to none (other than for those who had already booked Athens hotel rooms), the police weren't exactly wrong in their estimation of potential crowd size. Actually, they pretty much nailed it, whereas everyone else either severely undersold it or wildly underestimated it.

At the time, the Central Business District of downtown Athens was considered "active" when it had five thousand people walking around in it. It remained comfortable at ten thousand, but was considered to be at maximum capacity—meaning that zero vehicle traffic would be allowed—when crowds reached fifteen thousand to twenty thousand. By March 27, 1998—three weeks before showtime—the ADDA had increased its estimate of potential attendees to twenty-five thousand. The police department had, the above speculation notwithstanding, set its expectations at fifty thousand.

Lanier knew the crowd could easily wind up being larger than originally envisioned: "I tried to play it down because I could see that the police were getting nervous about this situation. So I think I told them not to expect more than thirty thousand people. I was obviously wrong. But I thought if I was, I wasn't going to say anything to that effect. So that's the [number] we started off working from, and as word got out about the show, they began to realize it was gonna be bigger than we thought."

At the time, the costs proposed by the police seemed outrageous at best to nearly everyone. In the end, the department probably barely squeaked by with what was required. Even so, Buck Williams recalled, "The police just couldn't grasp what was happening. They had this idea that we had all of these druggy hippies coming into town and they were not gonna be able to control it. I said to Gwen, 'These people have eighty thousand people out there every Saturday [during football season] partying their butts off. This is not gonna be even as bad as that. This is different because people are gonna be downtown and spending money everywhere. It seemed like the deal was a no-brainer, but the [police] kept adding and adding and adding. Then they'd add another ten police and then another ten. It just kept getting bigger and bigger."

Williams, who had been booking Panic in all types of venues for years, understood the importance of having an appreciation for both locale and culture. These are the things that make a place a *place* and not merely, as Williams said, a *market*. "I always look at Widespread Panic and compare it to a football game. The reason is, we play particular places all over the world. Wherever we play, they're particular places. And each and every place is specific to a venue and an attitude, as opposed to a market," he said. "Playing Red Rocks is very different from playing [Fiddler's Green Amphitheatre, in Greenwood Village, Colorado], which is also in Denver. And I think I sort of liken it to a football game because it's a gathering of alumni and friends from whatever school, and whenever the team plays, there's a huge amount of tailgating and prepartying, then there's the game, and then there's the after-parties. And that's the same thing that happens with Widespread Panic, 'cause that parking lot scene is where everyone gathers, and it really is a sort of a homecoming for so many people. And I thought that back in the days when we were planning this thing [Panic in the Streets], I said, 'I don't know what the big deal is. It's just like having a football game!'"

Sam Lanier echoed the football simile. "We were kind of comparing it in our own minds to a football weekend," he said. "At that time that meant seventy to eighty thousand people that would show up in town for a game including students, I guess. So, we were hoping to get there but we didn't wanna come across that way because we were afraid they'd turn us down flat."

Be that as it may, many other people had planned, well in advance, to hold events in Athens that weekend, and it's a fair bet that nary a one of them would have booked anything during a college football weekend. But even if the idea of conflicting events wasn't persuasive, there was still the matter of where to put people. Hotels, ballrooms, and meeting halls had been booked mostly solid for a long time for this weekend before Widespread Panic ever set its designs on the date. In addition to the Murray-Dillard wedding, Oby Dupree's cause célèbre, which was to happen just a block away from the stage, the Classic Center had ten events scheduled between Friday, April 17, and Saturday, April 18.

By the time every concern and controversy had been voiced and the entire conversation started reaching a fever pitch, Widespread Panic was just beginning a ten-day run at Paris's Chesterfield Café. Before that, the band had done a five-day run around Australia and an overnight stop in New Zealand. Never before had the boys traveled so far into open arms; ironically, back home some powerful arms were crossed against them.

"Right away there was a lot of 'Here's why you can't do it.' We were always about trying to make things work. [I'm sure] you've heard plenty of stories of how resistant and wishy-washy the city was," said Dave Schools. "Gwen was behind it, but there were other elements of the city ... aldermen that weren't into it. There was a whole lot of stuff, back and forth, that I remember leading up to it in the last few weeks. So we'd hear these little things, but we were out there doing what we do. It wasn't until we really got close to town that we realized what a hoopla it was. The city put up a lot of hurdles. We got a lot of that."

A more reasonable budget was written by city manager Al Crace. Totaling $61,250, it included $520 for fire marshal inspections of local businesses in order to prevent overcrowding on the day of the show, $4,500 for electrical services, $4,000 for solid waste collections and cleanup, and $52,500 for "Police, Sherriff and barricades."

Thus, the race was, as they say, on. It was up to the ADDA to counter this estimate but keep things reasonably in line. There was never any intention of underpaying for services or refusing to pay. But the higher the total price went, the greater the amount of earnest money and secured credit that would be required of Widespread Panic. The band knew the show wouldn't be free, but it's unclear whether they knew just how expensive it would become. "We had the weight of the mayor behind the event, but opposition started boiling up," Art Jackson said. "And although we have the verbal support from the county top, as we went through the process, new requirements kept popping up, and as soon as we solved one requirement, another hurdle would appear." As the formal applicant for the event, the Athens Downtown Development Authority was billing the day of the show as "Athens Music Day" and was able to bring it in as part of the Athens–Clarke County Community Events Program, established the previous year.

At first blush, this doesn't seem like a big deal, but the Community Events Program (CEP) was specifically designed to differentiate "community events" from "special events." The Central Business District of downtown had been the hosting area for multiple events of various sizes over the years, and the development of the CEP was formal recognition that, indeed, the streets were owned by Athens–Clarke

County (ACC), along with all the amenities they afforded. A commission agenda item from February 7, 1997, notes the ACC's ownership of trees and plantings, kiosks, light poles, bike racks, banner brackets, electrical supply systems, water and sewer utilities, benches, trash cans, and so forth. The idea was that the CEP could use these services during a series of planned events that would benefit Athens–Clarke County in ways that privately funded "special events"—for which ACC was only a permitting body—couldn't or didn't. The hard rub, though, was that anything done through the CEP put the ADDA on the hook for the entire bill. It was the ADDA's responsibility to secure all necessary funds to cover an event's cost. If an event didn't have funds allotted in the ADDA budget, it was the ADDA's job to find them from outside sources. The overarching and primary distinction between what constituted a "community" event and a "special" event was this: a community event had to be broad in appeal, enhance the image of the community, return a benefit to the community through tourism and visitation, and not be profit oriented.

For a CEP event, the ADDA acted as the sponsor or facilitator, the event was then formally nominated as a CEP to the mayor and the county commission, then it had to be approved by the commission in order to be placed on the county calendar of events, and then it qualified for supporting funds from ACC. For a "special event," on the other hand, one needed only make an application to Central Services, get approval from the relevant public departments heads (police, fire, solid waste), pay the costs as determined by those departments, and then it was off to the races. Special events could be profit oriented within specific parameters, and were under no obligation to promote the city's tourism or anything like that.

So why even bother with going through the ADDA and all the legal back-and-forth with the commission, city manager, city attorney, and others? Why not just pay the bill—which anyone doing an event would have to anyway—and be done with it? Well, for one thing, Widespread Panic needed advocacy. Athens Clarke–County is free to reject any application for a special event if it thinks the costs won't be covered or the event will be of such size and scope that the city can't properly contain it. The ADDA is specifically organized as a body of people, though, and isn't a one-person show. Even if the county commission were ready and willing to go along with what Art Jackson and Widespread Panic proposed, the plans would still need ADDA approval. Even with that small hurdle accounted for, it remained true that having the ADDA as an advocating agency, not to mention having the mayor on board, went a long way toward continuing a negotiation that could have easily been extinguished immediately.

Further, working with the ADDA was a sign of good faith on the part of Widespread Panic. It showed the band was being as transparent as possible with regard to what it wanted to do, but with no idea how to really go about it. So the band took it to the folks who would know. The first proposed budget under the newly formed CEP included the normal and known things like Christmas lights downtown, the UGA Homecoming Parade, and the newly created AthFest, which was still referred to as the Athens Music Festival. Under a section labeled "Spring 1998" was the notation "to be determined" and a target budget of $5,000. This figure would rise to $11,750 by the time of Panic in the Streets—an increase of 135 percent.

On March 27, city manager Al Crace sent a communiqué to Lorenzo Moss, chairman of the ADDA, taking the ADDA to task. Thus far, Crace said, the ADDA had not submitted a plan that specifically addressed attendance, the capacity of the CBD, law and ordinance enforcement, fire lane access, fire marshal inspections, medical services, public health, electrical services, parking, traffic flow, security and crowd management, and maps showing the full footprint of the event. Although documents exist showing that each of these items had been addressed either publicly or internally as early as February 17, Crace wanted them all, as the law required, packaged together as a "final plan of event management." In his role as city manager, Crace had the authority to deny the proper permits should this plan not be completed to his satisfaction.

By the time the government offices of Athens closed for business that day, Widespread Panic was six hours ahead, operating on Paris time, and in the midst of their tenth night in a row at the Chesterfield

Café. Back home, when the morning business of Athens–Clarke County resumed, the ADDA would begin its final scramble of putting together all the pieces for what everyone now agreed was a trip into the unknown.

6

MEETING OF THE WATERS

The original cost estimate of over $60,000 was a shocking, but not entirely insurmountable, figure. As it happened, though, it was also very much on the high side, even though certain parties seemed just fine with keeping that fact obscure. Practically no records exist except for one noting that the discrepancy was not acknowledged in the documents circulating at the time. It's literally proof of a negative, and thus the universe won that round. At certain points, it really felt as if the city was trying to price Widespread Panic out of its own self-created market. Everyone has a financial pain point, and there was always a possibility that point would be reached and Widespread Panic, Brown Cat, Capricorn Records, and the ADDA would just throw up their hands and say, "Well, we tried."

After this initial estimate was distributed, assistant county manager Phil Sutton sent a note to Mayor O'Looney, which read, "Please note that the specific reference to the $61,520 as a high end estimate *is not in* the final copy of this letter. We used $45,000 as a target expense figure with an acknowledgement that it could be adjusted higher or lower based on actual experience" (emphasis added). As a show of commitment and good faith, Widespread Panic delivered a check for $25,000 as a partial guarantee against costs. In short order, though, additional guarantees were required and the plans for the show could not advance without those funds secured. The initial twenty-five grand was "to show the commissioners that we were serious," said Sam Lanier.

"I think they were afraid they were gonna get stuck with some costs," Lanier recalled. "They were concerned about overtime for the police and medical staff and things like cleaning up afterward; they just didn't want to get tagged with the bill. It just took some convincing in the form of us putting up some money. From the commission's point of view, I think the budgetary concerns were the biggest thing."

The line-item expenses from Athens–Clarke County were guaranteed to the amount of $45,000 by the ADDA, and the financial records from the time are unclear about which expenses this money would cover. It is clear, though, that this amount did not include costs for further electrical improvements to the staging area, banners for light poles, and other expenses. Art Jackson did the math for everyone on April 5—thirteen days before showtime—and the amount was a jaw-dropping $107,700. This new figure included $35,250 for musical production costs (stage, lighting, etc.), which wouldn't have been included for a special event. But because this was an ADDA-sponsored happening, this disclosure was required and accounted for. Even though the ADDA, as the sponsoring agency, guaranteed $45,000 to the ACC government, the show was simply not going to happen without other sizable guarantees. A few days earlier, as the squeeze began to close tighter and tighter, Capricorn Records had stepped in.

Both Phil Walden Sr. and Phil Walden Jr. were very excited about this show, and senior, especially, had been in the business long enough to know what to ignore and what to take seriously. He had no problem in putting his money up when it was something he wanted to happen. "They were truly excited about it. They were gonna [film it] and record it. And Phil and Philip [Jr.] were both big into this thing," said Buck Williams. "This kind of fed into Phil Sr.'s ego. It was like he now had a band that was similar to his Allman Brothers days, when he had a band that big. Coming into Georgia and doing something of this magnitude? He was riding very high on it." Capricorn Records had a promotional budget of $50,000 for the release of *Light Fuse, Get Away*, and as was common for pretty much all major record deals, especially at that time, anything spent from that fund would be billed back to the band. Even so, Capricorn was more than willing to roll the dice in a big way and commit a majority of this money to the record release party.

On April 3, Wachovia Bank issued a standby letter of credit in the amount of $38,700 on behalf of Capricorn Records and named the Athens Downtown Development Authority as beneficiary. In turn, on April 8 the ADDA itself signed for an irrevocable letter of credit from First American Bank for $45,000 and named Athens–Clarke County as beneficiary. The guarantee from Capricorn was what the ADDA needed in order to approve an increase in the agency's own spending on Athens Music Day. The board members had resolved to raise its share to $25,850, but only if Capricorn came on board and secured the cost of all musical production requirements. Between the ADDA's letter of credit, its raising of its own spending ceiling, and the initial contribution from Widespread Panic, the city manager was satisfied that appropriate assurances were in place. The press had gotten hold of the story that the show might not take place and had run with it. Because much of the overall negotiations took place outside any legal requirement for transparency or record keeping, rumors sprouted from slight amounts of information and barely overheard off-the-record comments. On April 14—four days before showtime—a call came into the city manager's office from the *Atlanta Journal-Constitution* wanting to know whether "future events are going to be this hard to stage." Al Crace's answer was short but to the point. "The issue is the ordinance," he replied.

At the time, there was no legal differentiation in the application process for a potentially profit-making special event and an ADDA sponsored community event. The rules for each stipulated quite clearly that a "minimum of 30 working days" were required for "administrative review" of a completed application. This administrative review could happen only after the application had been replied to by the heads of each department that would be affected or needed for the event to happen. This meant after a full and complete application was made—including full plans for every aspect of event execution—it would then be sent around to the department heads and returned to the city manager's office with comments to be addressed. Only then would the clock begin to tick on the thirty-working-day requirement. For an event the size of Panic in the Streets the process should have begun much earlier than it did. Instead, the planning was off and running before it really had any legs. Although the show was announced on February 4, Art Jackson didn't begin filing formal applications until March 5, and the ADDA didn't vote to confirm a request for a special events permit until April 2, exactly one day before it had secured funds from Capricorn Records.

Al Crace had expressed from the beginning that everyone, including the ADDA, should be bound by the same legal requirements, and certain members of the county commission, while ostensibly supporting the same legal guidelines, provided Crace with a little back-slapping support, too. District 10 commissioner Cardee Kilpatrick wrote the city manager a note dated March 31 that said, in part, "I'm deeply concerned that we could end up footing the bill and I've expressed that to Gwen from the outset. I want you to know that I will support you in any way I can. I do not believe the taxpayers want their General Fund dollars to go into this kind of activity." At some level, Crace and the ADDA and the mayor were backed into corners, none of them comfortably. Crace had all the responsibilities with none of the overriding authority that had previously belonged to the mayor under the strong-mayor system, and Gwen O'Looney had all the vision and gumption to get things done, but was severely handicapped under the weak-mayor system.

Pete McCommons, editor of *Flagpole* magazine and cofounder of the *Athens Observer*, remembered the old system quite well. "One of the strongest mayors we've had in recent time was Julius Bishop, for whom Bishop Park is named," McCommons said. Bishop was Athens's longest-serving mayor, in office from 1964 to 1976. "He was a self-made man. He was wealthy, so he had his own personal power, but he was a kick-ass administrator. He just ran the government like he would run his own business. Basically did anything he wanted to. If he had wanted Widespread Panic, he would have just made it happen. He would have ordered the department heads to do whatever they needed to do. And he controlled the budget, so he would have said, 'Don't worry about the money.' He just had the ability to make something like that happen." It was this type of power specifically that delayed city-county unification for decades. "That's why they [adopted] the weak mayor[–council] system. The people in the county did not want to be under the thumb of a strong Athens mayor. The 'Athens mayor' was personified by Julius Bishop, and they didn't want any part of it." All of which is understandable, up to a point. Still, the glaring difference between the old ways and the new were brought to frustratingly crystalline clarity as planning for Panic in the Streets took place.

"The city had a lot of valid questions," said Mary Armstrong Dugas, office manager for Widespread Panic / Brown Cat, Inc. "They raised a lot of concern about having a concert downtown on the streets. That whole process [was] pretty intense and incredible. [I was] meeting with the university and [in] meetings with the city and other groups that were having events downtown. It just became quite a debacle."

Indeed, there may well have been a very good reason why Art Jackson didn't file formal applications for so long. Even though a solid effort was made to hit the ground running, soon no one could agree on anything. The tide began to shift solidly toward a final commitment and resolution only after the challenge to put up or shut up. Mary Armstrong Dugas got the call. She was attending a meeting with Sam Lanier, Gwen O'Looney, some commissioners, and other concerned parties. Dugas was called out to take a phone call, and on the other end was Brown Cat employee Ellie MacKnight, who had just spoken with Philip Walden. And he had just heard from Jim Marshall, the mayor of Macon, Georgia—coincidentally, the original home of Capricorn Records. Dugas called Walden back immediately, and he told her, "It's a done deal. Macon wants it. They're gonna sell beer, they're gonna make a big party for you, they don't care that it's last minute." After all the hemming and hawing and the muddled back-and-forth of Athens politics, a town that was basically an early second home to Widespread Panic was offering to foot the entire bill. "They were just gonna roll out the red carpet," said Dugas. "So I wrote all this on a piece of paper and walked back in [to the meeting] gently, and I slid the paper to Sam. And he just looked at me and rolled his eyes, and Gwen was, like, 'What's that? What's going on?' So I slid the note over to Gwen. And she busts out laughing so loud that it shut everybody else up. She said [to everyone], 'Well, that's it! We're gonna lose this. If we don't decide now about this, we're gonna lose it because it's gonna go to Macon.'"

"[The pushback] was amazing, because Athens had already begun priding itself as a music city," said Dave Schools. "And Macon, Georgia, was one of the first places outside of, say, Athens, Atlanta, and Greenville that we played. I remember the mayor saying, 'Hey, we love these guys. They got their start here! We'll be glad to host this street festival concert!'" But flattering and true as Mayor Marshall's sentiments were, and despite his supremely generous financial offer, taking the show to Macon was never seriously entertained. Widespread Panic envisioned the event as a gift to their town and fans, and well, Athens was home. "I never considered that, and I don't think anyone else would have either. This was a hometown thing. It just didn't make sense otherwise," said Lanier.

One man who was at the meeting made a poignant remark that has stuck with Dugas through the years. "And then I remember a gentleman saying, 'You know, we have to be careful of what we ask of people. People who want to do things in our city. Because if we ask this of them, we're gonna have to ask everybody the same thing," she recalled.

Several more rounds of memos went back and forth between departments, elected officials, and others before Al Crace finally issued an absolute deadline. Although the ADDA had met the city manager's deadline of April 3 for statements of financial assurance and the filing of a "letter of intent to file a final application", the absolute final line was drawn in the sand. The ADDA had until April 10 at five p.m. to deliver its financial instruments of assurance and guarantee, as well as cash payments, to the unified government, along with a final plan of complete event management.

Financial assurances were rendered two days early, on April 8, and the "Operational Plan of Action" was received by the city manager's office later that day. While a few bits and bobs of supplemental material were still needed, the submitted documents were enough for Crace to proceed. The next day, he wrote to ADDA chairman Lorenzo

Moss, "You are authorized to proceed with the event in good faith under the permit that is hereby issued." And just like that, nine days before showtime, Panic in the Streets was cleared for takeoff.

Quite oddly, the Taylor Murray–Mary Carroll Dillard wedding was little more than a tempest in a teapot when compared with the difficulty that event planners had with other factors. Indeed, that the press seized upon this story at all spoke less to the difficulty of accommodation than it did to the feel-good story of the year (namely, a free Panic show downtown) needing some tangible conflict for purposes of good storytelling. To keep the news train rolling, newspapers exploited every tiny aspect of this event and, in many cases, ramped it up to absurd degrees.

That may be a cynical and ungenerous perspective, but the press that followed this story with a microscope had motive, opportunity, and ability.

The mother of the bride, Carroll "Oby" Dupree, and the mother of the groom, Nancy Butts Murray, each had roots in Athens going back several generations. The man whom Dupree affectionately and casually referred to simply as "Uncle Dan," her mother's brother, was famed University of Georgia Athletic Department member Dan Magill. While still a student, well before his record-making achievement of becoming the winningest coach in NCAA history as leader of the UGA tennis team, he was a volunteer assistant football coach to UGA's famed Harry Mehre. Dupree's grandfather on her mother's side was Daniel H. Magill, an editor at the *Athens Banner-Herald* in the 1930s and 1940s. A great-grandfather on her mother's side was Eugene Winston Carroll, who in the 1920s sold the *Athens Banner* to the *Athens Herald*, thus creating the aforementioned. Her father's side of the family contained the legacy of the gigantic textile concerns of Wellman Thomas Textile—later simply Thomas Textile—which dominated Whitehall Road where the Oconee River cuts under it.

Nancy Butts Murray was a 1955 graduate of Athens High School, a University of Georgia cheerleading captain, and a graduate of the Class of 1959. Her father was beloved University of Georgia football coach Wally Butts. Although she left Athens for a long stretch during the two years immediately preceding the wedding, she was the house-mother for the Pi Beta Phi sorority.

The point here isn't to reduce this story to an Old Testament–style series of "begats," but to amplify the practically mystical confluence of events planned for April 18. Two of Athens's most prominent families, each with deeply sown roots and members known around the world, hosting nuptials on the same day—on the same street, even—as one of Athens's most prominent bands, one with its own brand of deeply sown roots and members known worldwide, hosting the world's largest record release party? For anyone believing that Athens was a place where anything could happen, this should have been proof positive. This much history coming together in the same town on the same street on the same day was truly mind boggling, even to those who thought that magic played a role in everything.

Mere weeks before the ceremony, though, it didn't feel like magic to the families involved. As is common in any place where folks live in the same town for years and years and grow up around all the same people, Athens could, and still does at times, seem like somewhere everyone knew everyone. In 1998, this was even truer. "The mayor was Gwen O'Looney, and I did not know Gwen," said Dupree. "When you're from a small town, and we referred to Athens at the time as a small town, you do feel like you know everybody. And it's an awful thing to say, because you feel like, 'We've got this covered,' because we know everybody, so we can do whatever we need to do. But I didn't know Gwen O'Looney, and she didn't know me." It is important to note that Dupree didn't mean storming about and getting her way simply through a small-town fit of who-knows-whom; rather, she meant that familiarity tended to clear up the process with regard to making an appeal. If you knew everyone, then you knew whom to call for help.

While news reports and internal memos circulated the notion that Dupree wanted the concert canceled or moved, she later said nothing of the sort was ever on her mind. The core problem that brought the two events into conflict was, actually, numbingly mundane. The wedding party needed clear access to the First United Methodist Church and some quiet time while the ceremony took place. The city needed the streets blocked off and made inaccessible to auto traffic in order to accommodate a gigantic crowd. Dupree may have not known O'Looney, but she did know Panic's office manager and de facto event negotiator, Mary Armstrong Dugas—then known as Mary Armstrong—and county commissioner Doc Eldridge. Dugas and the bride had gone to school together, and Dupree had gone to school with Eldridge. At the time, Dupree was working as the assistant to the editor at the *Athens Observer* newspaper. Although historically the *Observer* had been, generally speaking, a liberal alternative newspaper since its founding in 1974, by 1998 it had undergone a sale, a buyback by staff, and then another sale. It was by then a much more conservative outlet. It was the *Observer*, too, more than any other press outlet, that showed some sympathy to Dupree's cause. Hard-core ethicists might readily see a conflict of interest here, while others will simply recognize exactly how blurry the line gets with regard to small-town newspapers, interpersonal relationships, and editorial positions. "At the time, I was working for the *Athens Observer*, which was so coincidental," said Dupree. "I was the assistant to the editor there, which is also a joke, because I didn't know how to do anything. He was just a friend of mine who let me call myself that. But I'd work for him, and we had a good time . . . The bottom line is the *Banner-Herald* would have [negative stories] every morning. And I would be just about to die. For the *Observer*, we could sort of say, 'That isn't true!'"

The First United Methodist Church sits on the block that runs north-south on Lumpkin Street between Washington Street and Hancock Avenue. To the south is the Georgia Theatre, and to the north is the downtown Athens post office. The parking to the far rear of the church was, as mentioned, occupied by an old Athens police department filling station and a squat concrete building used for supplies and so forth. The rest of this property had already been reserved as a vending area for the Widespread Panic concert, and so was unavailable for other uses. The church's parking lot immediately to its rear was available, but would be made inaccessible by street closures, as would the privately owned parking lot across the street, which was impossibly small in any case.

More than any other issue surrounding the show, the wedding vividly caught the attention of the public. One particularly hot e-mail was sent to O'Looney by Sarah Kelly Jones, who at the time was working for the booking agency Madison House. "There are people from ALL OVER the country who have already made travel plans, hotel reservations, and adjustments in their schedules to attend this event," Jones wrote. "Why is it so difficult for this woman to accept the fact [the show] IS happening and try to work with the people who are bending over backwards to help her daughter have her special moment?" To revisit the concept of conflicts of interest: it's helpful to note that the Madison House client Big Ass Truck was scheduled to play that same day at Athens's High Hat Club, and the agency also represented, and still does, the jam band String Cheese Incident, whose fan base crossed over into Widespread Panic territory regularly. Everyone involved had a dog in this fight.

Commissioner Doc Eldridge, who would succeed O'Looney as mayor the next year, was fielding phone calls from concerned constituents far and wide making the case that someone needed to step up and take responsibility for all this, even if that wasn't exactly his job. In a private note not meant for public dissemination, he addressed the idea of moving the concert and brought up other items of note. "I am writing to *you* [Mayor O'Looney] as I do not want to make this into any more of a media story than it already is. I do, however, have some very real concerns," he wrote. "The wedding, I have to think, can be accommodated between concert times, parking, and shuttles (???). You and the ADDA seem to be trying to make things work. My primary concerns are 1) crowd size, public safety, and protection of private property 2) Financial aspect (the concert is 'free' but 'free' to who.) I realize this is a function of the ADDA but the general public looks to the elected officials for accountability and my phone has rung off the wall for the past week."

Although Eldridge's suggestion that the show could be moved to the old Athens fairgrounds out on Lexington Road came from a good place, anyone with any real knowledge of the band and its audience knew that Widespread Panic had long outgrown the days of the original Athens Music Festivals of the late 1980s and the multiple Super Jam events of the early 1990s. The band had played each of them, and even by 1994 its audience had packed traffic for hours as fans attempted to pile into the onetime carnival spot.

To this day, O'Looney carries no good memories of the wedding imbroglio. "The wedding! Oh my God, the wedding. I had no sympathy whatsoever," she said. Dupree, on the other hand, recognizes the hard spot that O'Looney was in. "She was in a horrible situation, you know, she really was . . . The whole thing was a mess. But I feel like I tried to get help, and at the time I was not happy that, you know, I didn't feel like I was getting help," she said. "But at the same time, in retrospect, what could they do? What could they really do? You know what I mean? Everything had already [been planned] . . . How could the town have said ahead of time, 'Well, we better make sure there aren't any weddings planned before we [schedule] this?' The negative side of it is that it was like the media wanted there to be trouble, and I hate to say that. I guess it's the way of the world. And it was a lie! I'm just being honest with you, but that's just a bald-faced lie. How would I think they could move a concert? How could they move the concert?"

Dupree had warded off or flat out refused to talk to the media almost every time she had the opportunity. "But the only conversation I ever had was with some man over the phone, and I can't even remember his name. I said to him, 'I don't have anything negative to say about Widespread Panic. I love Athens, Georgia," she said. "Did you know I was contacted by two Atlanta stations? I was contacted by *Time* magazine! And I told them I was very sorry, but I could not speak with them. And the two stations in Atlanta were channel 2 and channel 5, and they asked me to meet them on the steps of the First Methodist Church for an interview. I refused them, and I said, 'This is asinine. This is ridiculous. It is going to be resolved.' I would never do anything like that. And I never did. But you can pull up all this stuff. And I get tickled now [because one could read it] and think, 'That bitch!'"

In the end, of course, a plan was established that was generously offered by Widespread Panic and graciously received by the wedding party and their families. The wedding would go on as planned,

Widespread Panic would delay its start time by an hour, and city buses were hired to provide shuttle service for the wedding guests. Oby Dupree, to this day, lays profuse thanks at the feet of Mary Armstrong Dugas, Doc Eldridge, and Widespread Panic. Doc had been a family friend for decades, and the bride had been his children's babysitter pretty much from the moment they came home from the hospital. Plus, he had been married at the First United Methodist Church eighteen years earlier. "[He had] the idea 'why not let them use the buses?' And the city approved and thought it was a great idea. And I didn't know this, but other people can do that too," Dupree said. "He got a bad rap from a lot of folks that aren't Athenians who felt like he did that because we were friends and this, that, and the other. He did that because it was his job, and he would do it for any Tom, Dick, or Harry. He'd say, 'Let's try to figure this out.' And he came up with the idea, and he's that kind of person. He would help anybody. He's one of the finest men that I know. He's not a pretentious person. He tries to help everybody."

Once the arrangements were made, a notice was placed in the *Athens Observer* for those who might have received a wedding invitation, and then friends jumped on the phone to alert all the guests of the new plan. A significant number of guests were elderly, with limited mobility, so the shuttle buses were both a solution and a blessing. "But the biggest thing, to this day, that I cannot believe is Mary [Armstrong] Dugas and [her asking] the band [to move the start time] . . . Imagine Widespread Panic thinking, 'An hour? We don't know this girl you're talking about!' That was such a fabulous group of human beings. That they were all for it and wanted the wedding to happen," Dupree said. "The very first thing she did was announce that they were gonna delay starting one hour so that the wedding could be held. Now, that's big. That is big!" O'Looney recalled the band's flexibility as well: "The guys were so nice. They changed the [showtime] and, you know, waited until [the wedding party] had left . . . Really, they were great. They were great."

"It was all worked out so beautifully, I felt like God had his hand [in it] because I can't tell you how beautifully it worked out," Dupree said. "It really was unbelievable, because I am as easygoing and as easy to work with and get along with, and we all have different attributes. I was willing to do whatever as long as we worked it out to get there . . . And another thing is that never, not one time, did I have even a slight negative feeling about Widespread Panic. They didn't even enter into our minds. We loved Widespread Panic! We understood. In fact, one of my sons had other clothes under his tux so he could take it off and immediately slide out there to hear [the concert]. We never were upset with Widespread Panic. We were glad they were coming; we thought it was a wonderful thing."

Some readers won't understand why so much room has been dedicated here to a wedding. That's OK. There aren't many books about rock-and-roll shows that go deeply into, of all things, wedding planning. The reason for including it here is simple. The introduction to this book noted that for a huge number of fans in attendance that day, the popular idea is that Panic in the Streets just sort of happened. This idea reaches its absurd nadir with an idea expressed online. The author of the memory, while admitting he had a ball the whole weekend with nary a bad thing to say, gets everything absolutely wrong. "Widespread Panic set up stage in SAE's front yard [referring to the Sigma Alpha Epsilon fraternity], and all the fans loaded up on Washington Street for the show," he writes, as if the whole thing were just some super-casual thrown-together frat party. Nothing could be further from the truth. To repeat Dave Schools, memory is a manufacturing place.

But at the time, right at the tail end of the time line of possibility to get things in line, the Murray-Dillard wedding was set to proceed, the ADDA had its permits secured, and the money was in. Panic in the Streets was a go.

And it was almost go time.

TRAVELIN' LIGHT IS THE ONLY WAY TO FLY

As expected, fans began arriving a few days before the show. Early in the week, a telltale stream of barefoot and tie-dyed true believers started to flow into downtown Athens. The less crunchy fans—the ones the city had been promoting to naysayers as "Yuppie Grateful Dead" types—would arrive later. The back windows of the cars streaming through downtown Athens told a story in stickers that mostly read like code: "WP." "The Phil Zone." "Fukengrüven." "Love Your Mother." "Smile, Smile, Smile." Marijuana leaf decals of all sizes. And although legally indefensible with regard to the First and Fourth Amendments, it has always been open knowledge that if you don't want the cops to give you the side eye, don't cover your car with dope decals. A common joke from years ago went, "Nothing says 'probable cause' like a Grateful Dead sticker." In early 1998, it was difficult to believe that the oval black-and-white WP sticker wasn't having a similar effect for some fans.

Generally speaking, and with good historical evidence, police departments and rock-and-roll aren't exactly the best of friends. One side is charged with enforcing the law, and the other side has a tendency to flaunt lawbreaking—or, at a minimum, law bending—as a badge of honor. That said, the Athens–Clarke County Police Department isn't exactly known as a gang of head crackers looking for people to bust for little or no reason. The number of technically illegal social crimes they let slide, such as simple jaywalking and public intoxication, are positively legion during football-game Saturdays in Athens. It is a matter of prioritizing overall public safety versus writing tickets and making small-time victimless arrests. As the day of Panic in the Streets approached, though, rumors began to swirl about just exactly who was planning to come into Athens and what their intentions might be. The rumors ran from the truly bizarre to those based on fact.

At the time, Athens had a well maintained but rarely used mounted patrol, and Widespread Panic had to allay a certain fear with regard to the horses that would be serving on the day of the show. "At one point, someone raised a concern about 'dosing the horses,' about giving the horses acid. It was crazy!" said Mary Armstrong Dugas. Dave Schools said, "I knew we had a mounted police patrol, but you just didn't [ever] see them. But they were so scared that our fans were gonna lace the horse feed with LSD that we actually had to buy a new supply of horse feed in case that happened." It is entirely reasonable to assume that there was no chance at all of a Widespread Panic fan poking around police horse stables in advance of the concert, looking to turn on a bunch of heavyweight working steeds.

Other tales going around had a bit more weight behind them. In late March, less than three weeks before showtime, U.S. Customs agents in Memphis, Tennessee, intercepted a package of hashish that had been mailed from France to an address on South Peter Street in Athens. The agents sent the package to Customs agents in Atlanta, and the Athens–Clarke County Police picked it up from them. They made a "controlled delivery" to the named male recipient at the address and then made an arrest. During questioning, the suspect admitted he had mailed the package to himself from Amsterdam after being in France with some friends to see Widespread Panic. A police communiqué distributed on April 2 to select ACC personnel revealed some alarming news: "[The suspect] said that thousands from France are planning to come to Athens for the concert and that everyone is mailing drugs to Athens for the event. We alerted Customs to this and requested that they pay close attention to international packages coming to Athens." If anything were to strike concern into the heart of a small-town police department, this was it. Thousands of French people are coming! And they're all mailing drugs!

Of course, none of this was true, but no one can seriously blame the ACC for taking all of it as seriously as they did. Surely, if anything tragic with regard to controlled substances had taken place on the streets, especially if they had been made aware of the possibility, they would have been the first ones to take the fall. During the twenty-four hours immediately preceding showtime, rumors spread, with some evidence, that regional law enforcement departments were conducting safety and sobriety checks on the highways leading into town. Certain unnamed municipalities—conveniently located on GA-129 West—had been well-known speed traps for decades and didn't need any pretense for pulling cars over. "I remember [that on] the day of the show, or the weekend of the show, a lot of the county police or sheriff's personnel set up—now this is what I heard, I did not witness this, but I heard several accounts of this—roadblocks and little traps to catch people coming into Athens. You know, to see what they were carrying," said Buck Williams. "And from my recollection, they had three or four busts, but every one of them were local farmers who had nothing to do with the concert." These stories of law enforcement activity in outlying areas are still remembered by fans, too. John Gaither, one of those fans, recalled, "There was a lot of Athens-bound traffic coming from Atlanta. So somewhere along the way, maybe in Walton County, there was a sign that said something like 'Police License Check Ahead.' A fair proportion of the traffic was going to the Widespread Panic concert, and a fair amount of them were probably smoking marijuana. So a good number of those people turned off the highway onto a side road that was there, just after the sign." This elusive tactic proved fruitless, though, since fans were driving straight into the briar patch. "That's where the license check was, on the side road," said Gaither. "The sign on the highway was just a device to help the offenders select themselves and then deliver themselves to the law. That's the kind of trick that only fools you one time, but once is enough."

The Athens–Clarke County police, in coordination with the ADDA, had a huge plan in pace to address ingress and egress, crowd control, and traffic. "Downtown still had emotional and financial scars from [the] '96 Olympics, but AthFest in '97 had left a good taste in [the] community's mouth," said Art Jackson. "Several positives out of [the] Olympics [were that] Athens–Clarke County staff and the ADDA had developed some new guidelines and rules to help lessen [the] negative impact on downtown businesses, residents, cleanliness, and safety." The Event Management Plan went through multiple revisions as it was passed from department to department. Most of the changes from the original plan had to do with the legality of certain duties ascribed to volunteers and with logistical coordination. Overall, very little was changed.

The message was spread far and wide that the show would be a no-alcohol event. To this end, coolers would not be allowed into the concert area, and bars and restaurants serving alcohol were under extra pressure to keep their drinkers inside outdoor "café areas" they might have. Employees of each establishment were expected to be on high alert, check IDs (as the law required), and under no circumstance allow their establishment to become overcrowded. Anyone trying to bring a cooler into the venue area would have to leave it at one of five checkpoints that would be established for entry. Four of these points ran parallel to each other, north-south at the corners of Hull and Clayton, Hull and Hancock, Lumpkin and Clayton, and Lumpkin and Hancock. The fifth entryway ran east-west at the intersection of Washington Street and College Avenue, approximately four blocks from the stage and in between city hall and the downtown Athens parking deck. The heavy promotion of the event as alcohol-free may have been wishful thinking on the part of Athens–Clarke County, but was absolutely civically and legally necessary. In a memo to the county commission, Gwen O'Looney noted that the policy "sets a great precedent for our community in being able to host events that are cultural without being controversial." Addressing the legal aspects, Jared Bailey said, "The idea of making it a nonalcohol event with that many people there, and they're mostly college-age folks, yeah, it's wishful thinking no doubt. [But] it is illegal to drink on the street."

The question of parking, which weighed heavily on everyone's mind, had to be addressed. Athens was used to enormous football crowds, but over a third of fans lived in dormitories or parked at an off-campus residence. Much of the crowd coming to town for Panic didn't even know where local restaurants were. One might imagine that a regular cooperative relationship existed between the University of Georgia and Athens–Clarke County, but in reality, it didn't. Each maintained separate facilities, budgets, and police forces. Whenever one required something from the other, an arrangement had to be made. Before a plan of safety and accommodation could be securely in place, ACC needed assurances from UGA that those coming to town would have access to UGA parking.

Michael F. Adams, the newly installed president of the University of Georgia, earned his PhD in political communications from Ohio State University in 1973 and exercised his skill in this area brilliantly with regard to the needs of the city. He initially resisted supporting the downtown bar scene, which was developing as an antagonistic yet symbiotic component of the music scene. Still, he was keen to open up to the town and foster a good relationship between Athens and UGA. "On his first day at UGA, Adams went to the mayor's office. Not sure if that had ever happened before, but it did send a signal about warming town-gown relations," said Art Jackson. "But he also commented about how he wanted downtown to be more like Harvard Square [in Cambridge, Massachusetts] than Bourbon Street, which had not endeared him to the entertainment businesses. I visited Harvard Square a year or so later, and smiled when I saw the bars, staggering students, panhandlers, and dirty streets. I used to keep a gallon takeaway beer jug from Harvard Square on my desk!" Adams's cooperation and willingness to help accommodate travelers was instrumental to the success of the event and eased a lot of pain between the planners and authorities. "[We needed a certain] number of parking spaces available, more than we could ever handle downtown. A request went to Presidents Adams's office, and he agreed to keep their normal Saturday lots open," Jackson said. "[I] know President Adams was at the concert, [but] don't know how many people understood the significance of his support."

On April 1, UGA agreed to keep parking lots open in the same manner as it would for a football game. Parking for dorms and other housing would still be limited to those with a housing parking pass, which cut out potentially thousands of available spaces. Parking for recreational vehicles would be open on the East Campus at the

Ramsey Center and at a lot located on Hull Street as early as five p.m. on Friday, April 17.

Georgia Highway 316 had expanded four years earlier, so the east-west road now ran the full length between Interstate 85 and north-south GA-78. All those traveling this way would exit at 78, turn left, and then generally make the trip into downtown Athens by going straight down the road that begins as GA-29 and winds up as Broad Street. A goal was set to redirect this traffic, at least the RVs intended for camping, onto the Athens 10 loop around the city and then toward campus from the direction of South Milledge Avenue, from which drivers would need only to make an easy right turn to access the Ramsey Center parking. Similar directions would be in place for those traveling from the other main routes to Athens: 441 South, 78 West, 29 South, and 129/15 East. At final count, between the city proper and the UGA campus, approximately thirteen thousand parking spaces were available within a mile-and-a-half radius surrounding downtown.

Although UGA is known for its sweeping and lush North Campus area, as well as significant green space throughout campus, camping is specifically prohibited except in properly parked RVs. The university eventually allowed fans to sleep in their cars if necessary. Sandy Creek Park, located on the opposite side of downtown and up GA-441N, would be open for camping; before anyone had even shown up, they were expecting at least a thousand fans to spend the night. In an oddball confluence of events, on a weekend full of such things, Students for Environmental Awareness, which was holding its southeastern conference at the park, was fearful that attendees would skip out on conference-related events in order to see Widespread Panic.

In a very sweet move that simply flowed with the milk of human kindness, and was also akin to a raindrop falling into an ocean, the Athens Brewing Company offered floor space for one hundred people at a charge of only $15 a person. Because hotels were already booked to capacity, owner Brian Nummer was trying to help as many people as possible avoid lengthy, and possibly drunken, car drives to hotels in other towns.[1] The brewery's spots were offered on an unreserved, first-come, first-served basis. By the time crowds began piling into the downtown area en masse late on Friday night, urban camping was happening in nearly every available parking lot.

To be sure, some solo flyers were coming to Athens for the show, but for most this was a group event. Either caravanning or piling into the same vehicle, they hoped to have the biggest blast possible with as many people as possible. Lynn Rhodes came from Kinston, North Carolina, with a group of five, including her future husband. The long-time fan of R.E.M. had wanted to come to Athens for some time, and this was the perfect opportunity. She remembered their group "camping out beside a parking lot near the stage, and officials being kind and considering our safety." Needless to say, camping beside the stage wasn't part of the city's official plan. But just as UGA wound up allowing people to camp in their parked cars, the city eventually allowed the same activity and even, eventually, tolerated the existence of small tents set up in parking areas.

At the corner of Lumpkin and Washington Streets was the employee parking lot and drive-through teller service for the Citizens & Southern Bank. This proved to be a prime camping spot for those who arrived in time to claim a space. Besides being only two blocks from the stage, the lot was at a crucial central intersection allowing easy access to the rest of downtown. It was also mere feet away from the Georgia Theatre, which, for many fans, was Widespread Panic central. For this weekend, the parking lot would be WP central, too. Chad Saleska drove from Chattanooga, Tennessee, with a friend and arrived in Athens on Friday around five p.m. "We ended up parking our car for the weekend at a bank parking lot just as the employees fled for the weekend," he said. "We never drove the car again until we left Sunday morning, and this would be our base camp for the weekend, and soon others began to follow suit. We had a tent, lots of beer, and a bunch of new friends, and it was only Friday night. The later the night got, the more people started to show up at our bank, so it became something of a block party until the wee hours of the morning." He had just started heavily going to Panic shows the previous year, and the Athens concert would be his first in over three months. For regular music fans, this doesn't seem like any time at all to wait between shows, but for the Panic faithful it could be a miserable interval.

Cory Tressler, then a student at Michael Adams's alma mater, Ohio State, was turned on to Panic in 1996 by a roommate from Ottawa Hills, Ohio, which, he said, had "perhaps the largest contingency of Panic fans in Ohio." As soon as they heard that the band was releasing a live album and doing a free show, their plan was put in motion. Traveling in a caravan of six passenger cars and suvs, they didn't begin their almost ten-hour drive from Columbus, Ohio, until Friday.

"We rotated drivers, but I don't believe I drove on the way down. For reasons I can't remember, we drove through Pigeon Forge, Tennessee, and had a generally weird experience of being stuck in traffic [near] Dollywood!" he said. "We finally arrived in Athens after midnight and struggled at finding the camping locations, so we slept in the [1990s-era Chevy Blazer] with the air-conditioning on. We were awoken by a hippie pounding on the window, worried that we were dead, even though we were parked outside in the open air in a wide-open parking lot! Yes, we were young, excited, and stupid for sleeping overnight in a running car in the middle of a town, but there are much dumber decisions we could have made."

Indeed, there were. And of course, many worse decisions were made by many people in town that weekend. The overwhelming majority of memories most share from this time, though, contain elements essential to any rock-and-roll story, no matter the band or town in question. The combination of youth, adventure, excitement, a sense of possibility, a necessary measure of rebellion, a dose of recklessness, and a whole lot of spontaneity pretty much define the best rock-and-roll fans. Or at least the ones willing to do whatever it takes to have the best time all the time. The ones who will grab the moment, however temporarily and within whatever personal limits they self-prescribe, and decree their own personal pleasure dome.

For other fans, Panic in the Streets was something of a quest. The jam-band scene had lost a spiritual leader, and musical icon, in 1995 when Jerry Garcia passed away. While the current scene was in full swing by mid-decade there was no denying the long shadow the

Dead cast over everyone. (Only a few years earlier, the Athens band the Violets had taken a dark and humorous stab at hippie–and–Dead Head culture with their single "I Hate The Grateful Dead," which contained the chuckle-worthy, though obvious, refrain "I'll be grateful when they're dead!") For some fans, Garcia's death was a cultural passing of the guard. Dead fan Chuck Bertolina had only recently moved from San Francisco to Albany, Georgia, so that his wife could attend dental hygiene school. Panic in the Streets would be his first show by the band. "I have been a Grateful Dead fan for years, and after Jerry passed I had lost my music compass," he said. "I remember a good friend telling me to go to Athens on April 18 because a band called Widespread Panic was playing a free show in downtown, and it's an album release party for a live recording. I think his comment was 'I think they are exactly what you are looking for.'"

He packed up his motor home with his wife, Tanya, and their three-year-old daughter Andi and headed to Athens. They wound up parking and camping in the C&S Bank lot, which was, by then, swarming with fans. Anywhere one could find a car parked exhibiting the telltale signs of traveling Panic fans (road dirt, stickers, etc.), they would probably find at least one person sleeping inside it at some point during the weekend. Although no one reported camping, even car camping, on any church grounds, Athens–Clarke County had sought cooperation from the many churches located downtown. Athens's First Christian Church made its lot available for the volunteers recruited by the city to help with the event. To ward off in advance potential distress over litter being strewn around churches, Art Jackson sent out a notice on March 30 that promised the ADDA was committed to pay for all staffing and services necessary to ensure those attending church on the morning of April 19 would find the grounds of their places of worship clean. If churches were willing to do their own cleanup, there was a potential bonus to be had. "**MONEY CAN BE RAISED!**" said the notice (emphasis in the original). "Any church that is interested in selling parking spaces can easily charge up to $10 per space and have a ready fundraiser for one of your good causes. Of course, you would be responsible for your own clean-up but this worked great for many churches during the Olympics and would be a great fundraiser. Call our offices if you are interested."

Not for nothing, but the cleanup after PITS would be a veritable mountain to the Olympics' molehill. Not that anyone anticipated that at the time. With the crowd now estimated, mere days away from showtime, at a potential forty-five thousand, services would be stretched to their maximum but not necessarily overwhelmed.

Those who didn't sleep in cars, pack into the living rooms of newfound friends or longtime acquaintances, camp under the stars, or enjoy the rare, clean hotel room still occasionally got lucky. So to speak. Paul Eason and Erik Hammond drove up from Ruston, Louisiana. Eason had gotten his first taste of Panic in 1997 at the (now sadly demolished) Bronco Bowl in Dallas, Texas. "My friends and I were hooked!" he said. "I drove to Athens with my friend, and like an idiot college kid just figured we'd find a hotel or sleep in the car. Can't imagine doing that today. When we arrived, we were absolutely blown away! People were everywhere! We drove aimlessly around town, trying to find a place to stay. Everywhere we went was sold out. We arrived a motel that was a real dump, there were hippies juggling those sticks, and hula-hoop girls in the parking lot. I ran in and asked for a room. [The clerk] said they had one left, and I took it. It was more like a big closet with a bed. We were lucky to find anything!"

Except for some essential pregaming—which most would wind up doing in clubs, bars, or on the street over the course of Friday and deep into Saturday—there wasn't any reason to stick around a hotel room, anyway. No matter what one had going on inside a tent, room, or RV, everyone knew the actual party was out there. On the street. What had begun as a steady trickle of people turned into an ocean of humanity, and it was only a matter of time before the town would know whether it had sufficient sea legs. As the clock was striking the T-24 hours mark, everyone involved with the planning and execution of this grand experiment knew one thing: it had better.

VISITING DAY

As the sun came up on Saturday, April 18, 1998, the energy in the air was palpable. The plan had been to keep a closing schedule for each block of Washington Street in order to control vehicular traffic and ensure the city would remain as functional as possible for as long as possible. The block between Hull and Pulaski closed to auto traffic at three a.m. Soon afterward, the staging from Eastern Stage Production began to arrive, and sometime later, sound and lights from ESP Productions was on the scene. It was several hours until the band would be on-site, but that didn't matter. Everyone had plenty to do. It was gonna be a long day for the entire Brown Cat four-pack technical crew of Garrie Vereen, Dirk Stalnecker, Peter Jackson, and Wayne Sawyer.

Widespread Panic was a well-oiled touring powerhouse of a machine by this time, and a million miles away from the days when individual members toted their own gear to the gig, no matter how local. The Brown Cat offices were established in the old industrial row of warehouses on Foundry Street, and as the band and its general operations grew, this warehouse location—mere feet from the former locations of the Mad Hatter, Tyrone's O.C., and the Rockfish Palace—proved strategic as well. "When the band would come off tour, a semi would pull up to the Foundry Street space [and go into storage]," said Peter Jackson. "[On the day of the show] Garrie Vereen and I, along with members of the crew, put all of the equipment in the truck there at Foundry and moved it to the stage ... The band's equipment was all sort of fixed parts of an equation at that point. We were focused on that side of things."

Downtown retail establishments opened in anticipation of crowds of out-of-towners but were left with mostly browsing and bored folks looking to pass the time until Widespread Panic took the stage. The only shops doing bang-up business were the usual suspects for this type of crowd: any place that sold smoking accessories, T-shirts, stickers, CDs and records, and so forth. And although a clear warning had been sent to all tavern owners about potential overcrowding and the requisite policing of drinking on their premises, absolutely no one was prepared for the onslaught of hyperenthusiastic alcohol dollars. Before the afternoon was even in full swing, drinking establishments were running out of everything. The cheap stuff went first. Then, as top premium brands were being consumed just as quickly, some relief seemed to be in sight. The local beer distributors had made tacit commitments to replenish as many places as they could throughout the day. And they did the best they could, but most trucks were sent out with a single driver who would also act as delivery person. While there was, to be sure, a lot of love in the air that day, there was also the sneaky stench of opportunism. One poor driver did his best to load a delivery into the Nowhere Bar, right across from the Georgia Theatre. Not even a minute after he began pushing his overloaded dolly away from the truck, more than one person helped himself to a free case or so of beer. So exasperated was the delivery guy that he didn't even chase them. He just stood and sighed.

Kevin Sweeny, guitarist in the Athens band Hayride—notably, the only band in history to sign with Capricorn Records, split from the label, then re-sign with them—was tight with Dave Schools. In keeping with the dynamic of their friendship, Sweeny later said he most likely downplayed the possibility of Panic in the Streets being anything more than a normal, just more crowded, Widespread Panic show. "It was planned as an album release party, but we didn't know it was gonna become what it became. I didn't think it was gonna be that size. No one did," he said. "I thought it would be like the Human Rights Festival. Just a stage with a bunch of people around. I didn't think it was gonna be a massive influx like a football game. I can pretty much guess that Schools told us it was gonna be a big deal, and us just making fun of him for saying that. I know he would have mentioned it, and we would have been like, 'Yeah, yeah, whatever.'" As day turned into midafternoon, Sweeny knew he had been wildly mistaken.

The High Hat Blues Club, initially conceived as a blues and jazz joint, had opened about three and a half years earlier on West Clayton Street near the corner of Jackson Street. The owners and staff always had a sharp eye and ear for other styles, though, and it wasn't long before Americana, country, and rock-and-roll bands were occupying the stage at a rapid clip. Sweeny was working there in the spring of 1998. Figuring that there would be decent business that day, the club had a double bill of afternoon shows and night shows. The swollen crowd downtown was bubbling over into the areas past College Avenue, and Sweeny was completely taken aback when he tried to casually stroll down to see Dutch Cooper, a friend of his and Schools's who was pulling a shift at the tiny Engine Room bar down on Washington.

"We had an afternoon show, and a jam band played, and I ran sound for it. I don't remember who all worked that day, [but it was] probably all hands on deck," he said. "We set out from the High Hat, and there was a crowd of people. But by the time we got to Washington Street, it was impossible to walk through the crowd at all. It was just [so packed that] you couldn't get through." The High Hat crew decided to loop around the whole of downtown and try again. Taking the long route north toward Dougherty Street, they made a left turn there and headed down toward Hull—a mere block from the stage. It took them almost three hours to traverse the short block of Hull between Hancock and Washington. "As we passed the Manhattan [bar], I remember [longtime Athens artist and musician] Jim Stacy was there [holding down the door], and he was wild-eyed. We poked our heads in the door, and he was just screaming at people. They were selling entire boxes of beer. I remember him being like, 'This is insane. Like the worst football game ever.'" After finally making it across Washington to the Engine Room—a tiny but very long rectangle of a room next to the twenty-four-hour Jittery Joe's Coffee shop—they were out of luck again. "It took us forever. We walked in the front door, and it was the same scene there. Just complete mayhem. Our friends were crazed and couldn't even stop to talk to us. And we couldn't even get a drink from 'em," said Sweeny. They took advantage of a secret trap door behind the bar, exited through the basement, and started to make their way back toward

West Clayton Street. There was still a night show they had to work. "We thought, 'Well, fuck it. We're not gonna see our friends, and we're not gonna see any music,'" he said. They took in a treat of stuffed filet mignon at the New Orleans–style restaurant Harry Bissett's, caught a catnap in the booth, and then headed back to work. Sweeny does remember seeing Engine Room owner Mike Church looking up at the roof of his establishment and yelling at a crowd member to come down because it wasn't safe. The woman in question looked right back down at him and yelled, "I'm the mayor!"

It wasn't just Gwen O'Looney who was looking for refuge and a good sight line that afternoon. Several people had been granted, or had granted themselves, access to the contiguous roofs of the buildings on the eastern side of Washington between Pulaski and Hull. Most were folks known to the establishments under those roofs, and it seems the majority gained roof access through the 40 Watt Club.

Because of limited space immediately behind and around the stage, the 40 Watt served as both a backstage and a dressing room area as well as a sort of command center for the Widespread Panic management team. Although the staging, lights, and sound were all set up and pretty good to go well before showtime, there was a storm brewing just outside Athens that threatened the whole event. "There was a small television we had inside the 40 Watt, back in the office, to watch the Weather Channel," said Mary Armstrong Dugas. "I remember Sam and Buck and Phil Walden all huddled around the [TV], looking at the radar, watching this storm come across Georgia. And they kept saying, 'It's coming, it's coming.' I mean, [we were] literally on pins and needles just waiting for it to get close enough to pull the plug."

Not that anyone on the street had any idea of this. For the assembled crowd, the party was already in full swing. Ryan Cook, an under-twenty-one kid from Marietta, Georgia, made the trip up with a friend. With an older brother attending UGA, he was used to making the journey and knew the town well. And although he and his compatriot lacked the standard-issue fake IDs most kids tote around town, they had other plans. "We were downtown most of the morning and afternoon that day, just kinda fucking around because we were underage without fake IDs," he said. "But [we were] avid Widespread Panic fans nonetheless. We both dropped our first [dose of LSD] at, like, ten a.m., and by two we had already taken three hits. I think we got a bad batch or something, because the trip only lasted for, like, four hours after we dropped, like, three hits of acid. Those four hours, however, were amazing."

Chad Saleska, who had staked his camping claim the previous night at C&S Bank, said, "That morning I went to check out the stage. It was interesting seeing it with virtually no one there and then again once completely flooded with people later in the day. It had an eerie sense of calm, though the buzz was certainly in the air. We went to the stage pretty early to get set up, and I remember sitting down and smoking copious amounts of weed as we waited."

While the locals worked, and the out-of-towners partied, more than few Athens families brought their kids down to see what the big deal was. A solid contingent of Athenians always gets into the spirit of civic happenings even if they aren't totally in line with their tastes. At the time, Marina Doneda was twelve-year-old Marina Edwards, and her parents brought her downtown. They were a couple of the original founders of the Athens Folk Music & Dance Society, and Edwards was accustomed to attending concerts and such. Once they arrived at the concert area, Edwards and the friend she had brought with her were allowed to just go explore. "Thinking back on this now, I feel like my parents were crazy to allow us to do this! We were twelve years old, and there were a hundred thousand people in town, and they just let us go free," she said.

Brenda Mallonee's son Joseph was only eleven years old but deeply familiar with the Athens music scene. His father, songwriter Bill Mallonee, was a staple of the folk-pop scene with his band Vigilantes of Love, and Joseph was exposed early to much of the music of Vic Chesnutt, Neutral Milk Hotel, Bloodkin, and others. The young Mallonee was excited to take a stroll downtown with mom to catch the show, and they positioned themselves atop the parking deck at College and Washington. This would be Joseph's first Widespread Panic show. "I peered out over the parking garage's railing and saw thousands of people who gathered together for one purpose," he said. "We were all in one place to groove, spin, noodle, shout, sing, and rock-and-roll, [and that] would end up becoming a lifelong obsession of mine. Sure, I didn't know one word to anything that was played, but that didn't matter. I felt the power, I felt the love, I felt what it was like to be a part of something."

The band itself was pretty removed from the goings-on in the street. John Bell was due at UGA's Foley Field in the early afternoon to sing "The Star-Spangled Banner" before the Bulldogs' baseball team played the Kentucky Wildcats. Less than two miles from where tens of thousands of people were gathering to see his band play, Bell found himself singing to a gathered crowd of sports fans who were not necessarily Panic fans. "That was my first national anthem, and I was nervous as all get out," he said. "Buck [Williams] and I went over there, and, yeah, you know, it's a college game. It's not like there were a lotta fans. There were some, but it was a little out of my wheelhouse. I really, usually, don't experience nerves, and I definitely didn't at that point in my career. So that was a new feeling. It was the same feeling I had right before I got married. I was like, 'Oh, wow!'" By showtime, he was all smoothed out. "I used up all my nerves that day, so when it was time to do the gig, it was cool."

Dave Schools had spent the previous forty-eight hours focusing on the mundane but supremely important task of moving into his newly purchased house. The need for some renovations had prevented him from taking care of the move before the band went overseas. The work was done while he was on tour, and even though he was due to appear in the biggest thing to hit Athens since the Olympics, this was also his moving weekend. Indeed, he had been so busy with house planning that he hadn't even had time to really think about the gig itself and all the issues surrounding it. "There was so much stuff going on. The normal stuff of being on the road and then dealing with a house move. I just didn't have time to think about it. Obviously, we had no idea that many people were going to show up. We didn't have a clue. We were thinking twenty thousand, but I don't even think about things like that," he said. "After about two thousand—when you can't see people's faces in the back—it's all one amorphous thing. So it was just shocking. And to top it off, I was moving! I'd been living with Ellie and Robert MacKnight." Enlisting the help of longtime friends when moving was, and is, such an Athens tradition that even when one could conceivably hire movers, no one generally did. "Literally the night before the show, Dutch [Cooper] came with his pickup truck and helped me move the meager possessions I had—which was mostly CDs and vinyl [*laughter*] over to the new house." As he fell into bed on Friday, less than one full day before the show, he could hear the sound of bongo drums from campers at nearby Sandy Creek Park.

Public access television—known as PEG programming, for public, educational, and governmental—was hot in Athens from the moment it became available. Rabble-rousing scenester Chip Shirley spent a few years in the 1980s making his show *Partyline* in the studio of Observer TV, which was owned by the *Athens Observer*. Back in Athens in 1998 after a nine-year absence, he was pitching a new show, called *Scope*, to the local cable company, so he set out with a less-than-stellar camera—he said the company's good one was already rented—and hit the street. His evening footage shows the impassable crowd from a street-level view and functions these days as a moving snapshot of what it was like downtown that night.

Earlier in the day, musician Kitty Snyder was in the midst of covering the event for the local TV show *Sound Check*. She had been hired to regularly host the program by show producer Theodore Radford, who had done a segment on her band Loveapple and liked the way she presented herself on camera. Around three p.m. she joined Dave Schools on the roof of the building housing the Hole in the Wall bar to grab an interview. "The crowd was beginning to look a lot bigger than we originally anticipated, and we needed somewhere to film where we could look down upon the crowd and get that exciting perspective for the camera, as well as get some space for the interview," she said. "At the intro to our episode, it was hours before the show, and there were already so many people in the street waiting for the show. But by the time the show started, there were exponentially more." Schools was relaxed and cordial, surveying the crowd through sunglasses. As the crowd on the street recognized him, he smiled broadly and waved down as deafening cheers rose up. In her interview, Snyder hit her journalistic stride when she said to Dave, "The newspapers have been really diligent lately about reporting all the problems and concerns surrounding this concert. One of which was the wedding. Another one was Capricorn having to give a certain amount of money to provide the right police protection and everything. And it didn't seem like it was gonna happen for a while, and everybody was all worried. Did y'all have any concerns about this, or were you pretty confident it was gonna happen, no matter what?"

Schools had already answered similar questions for local and regional papers, including the *Red and Black* and the *Athens Banner-Herald*, but he was still polite and gracious with Snyder. Indeed, exhausted as he may have been with the subject, he seemed pleased to answer. "Well, we were in Europe when the whole wedding fiasco was going on. We got back just in time to give [the city] a deadline to give us the permit, which was last Thursday at five o'clock. Otherwise, we were gonna go do the show in Macon because they offered it to us free of charge." More than anyone else in the Panic camp, Schools seemed to take the most umbrage at the city's protracted way of negotiating. This wasn't really surprising, though, since Schools was, by far, the member with the most pronounced punk rock, "let's do it" personality in the band. If any member was likely to say "Why not?" at any stage of the city's pushback, it was going to be him. "Personally, I'm really not surprised, because it is a small town and everybody knows everybody. Everyone that lives here chooses to do so because it's a small town. We all like that aspect of it," he answered. "We certainly don't have any plans to have thousands and thousands of people come and trash the town. We hope thousands and thousands will come and appreciate what a great town it is and [understand] why we choose to be here and live here."

Photographer Wingate Downs, an Athens resident since his student days began in 1977, was hired to shoot both the concert and the surrounding event. He said it was a fairly standard plan, but with the addition of aerial photography. The low-hanging cloud cover was a challenge to overcome, but through some quick law bending he got the shots he needed. He usually used single-engine Cessna 170s for aerial work. He would shoot out the window and right over the wing. "I'll tell you, though, that was an interesting day, because the [cloud] ceiling was really low. I think five hundred feet is the lowest [pilots] can fly over a populated area, and we were pushing it," he said. "I think [the pilot] may have dipped down just because I needed it. I couldn't see because of all the fog. I couldn't really see what I needed to see. But we [only] made about two passes because it just wasn't a comfortable thing."

Backstage, right in the heart of the production, Peter Jackson surveyed exactly what the crew was working with. "We were fucked down on that stage. It was just the most underfunded, unplanned-for thing," he said. "We had no professional stagehand labor. It was the sound company representatives, lighting company representatives, the stage company, but, you know, [there were no] IATSE—International Alliance of Theatrical Stage Employees—stagehands…We had the band's crew and the professionals from the vendors, and that was it. All of the stagehand labor was, like, volunteers. Somebody in the brass ranks thought, 'Oh, well, we'll just get a bunch of volunteers to do it. Some college kids or whatever. They'll love to do that.' So we're putting together this production that—from the [perspective] of the band's history and everybody that had worked for them—this was by far and away the biggest thing any of us had ever done. And it was done on a goose egg of a budget."

Indeed, the mayor had put out a call for volunteers to help with various tasks, and some of those jobs dovetailed nicely with the charitable spirit of Widespread Panic. The band had specifically requested that folks attending try to bring some canned goods for the Food Bank of Northeast Georgia. And oh, did they! Volunteer Hal Turner said, "My actual assignment on the day was working a collection table for the food bank. Throughout the afternoon, so many cans of food appeared. One team rolled up with a hand-truck and stacks of cases." Dave Schools noted that the band was clearly of the "think global, act local" mindset. "You know, everything we did up to that point, any charitable contribution, we always kept them local," he said. "We supported the Women's Crisis Center, we supported the food bank. You know, we're pretty serious. We followed the lead that R.E.M. gave, which is [to] really support the place that you're from. And we were proud to be from Athens. We loved Athens."

The gathered families and friends inside the First United Methodist Church loved Athens, too. The parents of the betrothed couple were well acquainted with large, football-style crowds, but by the time the wedding was under way, the gathered throng for Widespread Panic was well past the fifty-thousand-person point. Even with the agreed-upon accommodations in place, anyone would have been a little apprehensive. As promised, though, the band had spread the word far and wide to their fans that quiet around the church space would be very much appreciated. No sound was broadcast from the stage for the duration, either. What happened next still gives goose bumps to Oby Dupree. "The neatest thing was as soon as the wedding was over, when my daughter and her newlywed husband walked out, the crowd saw her, of course—because she was in her bridal gown—and started roaring and shouting and clapping," she said. "And the groom did a thumbs-up to 'em and helped the bride into the car and they took off. It was the neatest thing! It was wonderful."

It was almost time. The sound was fired up onstage, and the first song played over the speakers was "Black Jacket" by Panic's longtime friends and collaborators Bloodkin. Though Jackson bemoaned the lack of pro stagehands that day, there was one person present who was more than willing to sweat it out with the best of them. Steve Fleming, who had been head of security and doorman at both the Uptown Lounge and the Georgia Theatre, knew Widespread Panic like family. So he knew—just knew—on the night in 1992 when JoJo Herman tried to get into the gig without a ticket, claiming he was the band's keyboard player, that something wasn't right. Terry "T" Lavitz was the band's keyboardist, and Fleming had just seen Lavitz drinking at the bar. Eventually, Dave Schools smoothed everything out and vouched for JoJo. Thus, the story of "One Armed Steve" was born. And there was no way he was going to miss seeing the boys play their biggest show in Athens.

"As the concert approached, I realized from talking with Sam Lanier that the only way that I was going to be able to see and enjoy the concert was to work on the crew. I volunteered to be a roadie for the show," he said. "After unloading the trucks and helping set up the stage, I settled in just off of stage left to enjoy the show. Then Garrie Vereen came up to me and asked me to come with him, as the band wanted to talk to me. I followed Garrie to the front doors of the 40 Watt Club, and all six band members came through the doors and encircled me. I was thinking like, 'What the hell is this all about?'"

In pure polite Panic style, they wanted his permission to play "One Armed Steve," a song they had written about the seven-year-old incident. Sure enough, the band would begin the night's second set with it. When Fleming went back over to his spot at the front side of the stage, Michael Stipe—who had been hanging around in the same spot, chatting with him—said, "Now you know what it feels like."

The band was ebullient, but knew it had a job to do. The crowd was swelling toward what would be a reported eighty thousand to one hundred thousand people. To put this into the sharpest perspective possible, the entire population of Athens–Clarke County didn't number 100,000 in 1998. "The moment of fear that I experienced was stepping onstage and looking out at all those people. [It] was like, 'OK, we have a really big responsibility,' and I'd never looked at it this way," said Dave Schools. "But it was like, 'We have to do our job and keep these people engaged. Keep 'em focused.' Because if they were to become unhinged . . . You know, it could be terrible."

Peter Jackson and the rest of the Brown Cat foursome were in position onstage as the band walked on. Less than five minutes would elapse before they made history. "As the guys came up, they kind of all huddled on the stage," he said. "You could just feel the childlike joy of what they were experiencing. It's tough to think about Michael [Houser] not still being around. It's choking me up [to think about it], but they were just like children up there. [They were] so happy."

At the sight of seeing the band gathered together, the audience roared in appreciation, approval, and anticipation. There was just one thing left to happen before Panic in the Streets was a complete reality.

9

RAISE THE ROOF

The most galvanizing and memorable moment of the entire week-end belonged to Gwen O'Looney. She had been this event's most vo-cal and public cheerleader, working as hard as possible from a posi-tion of little political power. And now it was all happening. Before Widespread Panic struck its first note, she stood proudly on the stage and announced: "Welcome to Athens, Georgia, home of Widespread Panic!" Then she spoke her most memorable statement of all: "Don't hurt my town!"

The faithful were at the front. As soon as the gates opened at three p.m., they had made their way—some making mad dashes—to be as close to the band as possible. Now, after almost five hours of lounging and waiting, it was happening. The only show in Athens that was both contemporaneously fabled and simultaneously battled was about to happen. At eight p.m. the air was a comfortable 65 degrees Fahrenheit, but the 88 percent humidity was magnified substantially by the num-ber of bodies present. If you happened to be within the first block of the show, you weren't going anywhere. Every available surface on the ground was taken, and folks started climbing up on a garage used by the Snow Tire Company, crosswalk signs, light poles, electrical boxes, and anything else they could use to grab a better view. Herbie Andrews was a high school senior from Florence, South Carolina, and he recalled, "Once we got to the street, people were everywhere. Our crew kind of got lost and dismembered [sic] in the madness. I somehow—not even really sure how—ended up on a rooftop on the right-hand side of the street. There were about ten or fifteen people already up there. I was thinking I would be watching the rest of the show from up there. It wasn't long before the Athens police asked us to get off the roof."

These weren't the only rooftops the police were watching, either. As part of the event management plan, they were set up in strategic positions all around the concert area. In retrospect, there may have been a certain amount of undue caution in their plan, but without being in their specific role that night, it's difficult to lay any blame. The most intense level of their plan was never observed by the general public, but the details are sufficiently chilling. "The police, who I did have to deal with, were very concerned with this event. About being able to provide public safety for a large number of people, deal with the traffic, and they were also concerned with the amount of drug usage that might be going on," said Jared Bailey. "They had the GBI [Georgia Bureau of Investigation] there. I think they had helicopters. They literally—and I saw this with my own eyes when I went up to the rooftop of the Morton Theater—had snipers up there watching people in case there was a problem. It was overkill. They were videoing people and everything. They had the snipers in case there was an event, but they also had people watching the crowd. I mean, they had guns and were in sniper positions, but they weren't training their guns on anyone. But I went up there and I saw it with my own eyes."

Eventually, the concern for public safety took precedence over any routine patrolling for alcohol and small-time drug offenses. If things went even a hair in the wrong direction, a whole lot of people could have been seriously injured. The psychology of crowds is a tricky thing, and the combined forces of self-preservation and deindividuation (that is, when members of a crowd, specifically because of their membership in the crowd, become separated from their individual identities and assume anonymity) can be the twin fists behind any number of unwelcome behaviors. It was better to just try to keep everyone as cool-headed as possible than to start busting some college kids for passing a joint.

"You gotta remember that folks involved with the police . . . most of them are former military, and they get very uptight about that sort of stuff. And they think they've got to plan for the worst-case scenario instead of thinking, 'Oh, well, there'll probably be a few people smoking pot,'" said Bailey. " Instead, they've got to get very intensely prepared for it. That's the mindset of the military, you know? [But] at a certain point, the police decided they were going to be more concerned with the larger safety issues than alcohol consumption or small-time drug use."

Athens had long been a place where smaller communities could schedule events like conferences, training weekends, and the like. At the time, it was also a popular destination for area high schools to hold their proms. Loganville High School was lucky enough to be having its prom at the Classic Center that night. It was practically comical how the planners romanticized complete disaster by choosing "Titanic" as their theme that year. Presumably, other equally appealing themes— "The Towering Inferno!," "Potato Famine!," "Earthquake!"—were already taken. Sure enough, more than a few Loganville kids snuck out and checked out what was happening. Senior Heidi Malloy and her date took a stroll down to the area to check out what was going on, but were self-conscious of their formal wear. "We feel like dumbasses, actually", she said.[1]

Athens as a town had undertaken a project of herculean proportions and was pulling it off. The band would be back on the road only a few days later, celebrating the new album's release with multi-day runs through familiar venues and towns. Eventually, they would hold the record for the most sold-out shows at Colorado's Red Rocks Amphitheatre. But here, at this time and in this moment, on the streets of their hometown, they were doing the unrepeatable. Right there on Washington Street, the birthplace of flight in Athens—mere feet from Ben Epps's second airplane shop and only two blocks from their cradle, the Uptown Lounge, and their beloved Georgia Theatre—they were making history. Nothing of this scope would take place in Athens again, and Widespread Panic would never again attempt it. Collegiate sport victories and the university being named multiple times as a "Top Party School" in the United States notwithstanding, the biggest mass-cultural record the town could wear as a feather in its cap happened on March 7, 1974. That was the day over one thousand university students held the biggest streaking event in the nation. The excitement for it was such that the streets were lined with coolers and beach chairs full of spectators taking in the view.

When Widespread Panic began playing—right after John Bell's enthusiastic greeting, "Evenin', ladies and gents! Welcome to Athens, Georgia!"—it was the culmination of many things. It was more than a band playing a gigantic free show. Lots of bands had done that. It was more than a homecoming, too. Panic had been made of road dogs from the word go, and the concept of homecoming was long-familiar language to them. This was a victory.

Light Fuse, Get Away was assembled from a handful of live shows recorded the previous year, and a regular band would have mimicked those sets for a release show. Widespread Panic wasn't a regular band, though. The only songs to appear on both the record and during Panic in the Streets were "Disco," "Porch Song," "Love Tractor," "Pilgrims," and "Space Wrangler." Although the band chose at least a portion of the set to specifically appeal to longtime fans from Athens, their well-noted process of designing set lists so that no song would be played more than once in three shows was at work, too.

The sun was slowly setting behind the stage as the night opened to eruptions of cheers and the band dropped right into the swinging, shuffling riffs of "Disco." The area immediately in front of the stage, which had been a de facto lounging area all day, was packed tighter than shoulder to shoulder. As the music began, the release of energy from the crowd was so explosive that it was if they had finally been given permission to let go. The fists pumping in the air signaled an effusive joyfulness that would mark the rest of the performance. Unsurprisingly, the combined effect of travel, heavy anticipation, and, for more than a few, a long day of heavy partying wound up rendering the actual performance a blurry good time of celebration and familiarity. Thank heavens, then, for those who had the foresight to capture the show on film and tape. While complete audiotapes of the entire show include over twenty songs, the official record provides a mere ten. The full set was a dealer's-choice selection. It ran, in order, as follows:

Set 1: "Disco," "Tall Boy" > "Love Tractor," "Aunt Avis" > "Diner" > "Walkin' (For Your Love)," "Henry Parsons Died," "All Time Low," "The Take Out" > "Porch Song" > "Blackout Blues"[2]

Set 2: "One Armed Steve," "Chilly Water," "Greta" > "Christmas Katie" > "Radio Child," "Arleen" > "Papa's Home" > "Drums" > "Papa's Home," "Pilgrims," "Fishwater"

Encore: "West Virginia" > "Space Wrangler," "Ain't Life Grand"

Though edited, the proper releases, which came out on film and audio in 2002 (each named, of course, *Panic in the Streets*), are thoughtful with their selections and serve as a fine primer for anyone who wasn't there, and a decent reminder for those who were. For others, they help confirm stories bandied about as legend among friends.

"Toward the end of the second set, I had made my way between the stage and the security railing for the general public. Not sure if I was in a VIP area or just a buffer zone," said Herbie Andrews, who came from Florence, South Carolina. "When the boys came out for [an] encore, Dave whistled 'West Virginia' before they broke into 'Space Wrangler.' Dave whistled 'West Virginia' staring right at me, and gave a nod and a smile afterward. Out of the hundred thousand people that were there, I was able to live that. On the way home, I told the crew what happened. Of course, no one believed me. Once the VHS tapes came out, they were believers." For others, specific moments stand out more than others. Maggie Shuff, from Nashville, Tennessee, swears she can't remember the bulk of any set list even immediately following a Panic show, or identify most songs by title at all. But of this night, she said, "I do remember one song from that night because timing was spot on. It was hot, muggy April . . . They struck the chords of 'Ain't Life Grand,' and it started to shower! It was a nice, soothing, cooling rain, and it went perfect with [my] need for a fresh breath."

Hard-core fan Chad Saleska, from Durham, North Carolina, could barely keep up his diligent note taking because of the tightly packed crowd and generally buoyant atmosphere. "We were actually pretty close to the stage, way off to Mikey's side. It was the first set of trees back, and I used the trunk of the tree as a shield against the crush of humanity behind us," he said. "It just felt like a culmination of energy, a rock-and-roll coronation, a fucking dance party. Way back then, we'd write the set list on pieces of paper. That all went to hell when the band debuted 'All Time Low.' I think I called it 'Reaper Man' when I wrote it down, because those were the only words I could make out. When I didn't know the name of the first song of the second set ['One Armed Steve'], I stopped trying to keep up. Then [the band debuted] 'Christmas Katie.' In the hundreds of shows I have seen since, I am not sure I've seen three debuts of new material [in one show]."

Scott Kegal had first come across Panic at his Davidson College fraternity house during a party in 1989. In 1998, though, he was a veteran of over sixty shows, and he made the trip to Athens with some buddies from Charleston, South Carolina. "There were people on top of buildings, hanging out of windows, clinging to telephone and electricity poles . . . But no one seemed to care about anything but the music," he said. "The band played a new song that I had never heard, with what appeared to have a chorus of 'My principles are reaching an all time low.' The band relished delighting the crowd with this new tune. Shortly thereafter, they left stage and returned for second set. The second set was awesome but seemed to fly by, and the band once again left the stage for a short break and returned for the encore—closed with JB toting the mandolin, and everyone knowing 'Ain't Life Grand' was coming. JB and the entire band and crowd whooped into a frenzy as the show came to a conclusion. I recall thinking to myself that life was pretty damn good at that moment and that I had just experienced another unbelievable live music performance."

Jason Key, a fan who came down from Chapel Hill, North Carolina, related a strikingly similar experience. "The best memory for me was the encore," he noted. "It started to rain a bit during 'Wrangler,' I think, and by 'Ain't Life Grand' it was really coming down. Everyone was loving it! The joy and happiness of one hundred thousand people dancing in the rain was truly magical. The speakers near us were going in and out toward the end, which was crazy and made the whole thing seem even more epic. What a day, what a show!"

When it was all over and the air cleared, more than enough people were patting themselves on the back, regardless of any initial objection they may have had to the whole thing. Dave Schools could smell it a mile away. "Everybody definitely learned a lot. And the thing is, even though it was the band's idea, people have circled back around. There have been a lot of circle backs like, 'Let's do it again!' And they're coming from people who were kind of naysayers [during] the first instance," he said. "And I would be the one, and I don't know how many other band members or management team members would agree with me, to hold that it worked out as best as it could. Let's not eff it up now. Let's not do it again or make some tradition out of it, where the odds of something going wrong or people being like, 'How can we make money off of this?' increase to a greater extent."

The Athens Regional Medical Center had ambulances in key positions around the concert area. It's an honest miracle that no one was badly hurt or injured, and if that sounds hyperbolic, think of it this way: the assembled crowd matched or exceeded the entire population of the town. On any given night, a few emergencies happen. For nothing of the sort to happen in such a condensed area was miraculous. In the final event review and analysis, it was noted by the ACC Police that three people were treated for acute alcohol toxicity at the Athens Regional Medical Center. Of these, an eighteen-year-old and a nineteen-year-old had severe but normal symptoms. The third, a fifteen-year-old girl, had a blood alcohol content of .32, which is deadly for a person of any size. She survived.

Most of the final police report focused on the demoralizing aspect of the inability of the assigned officers to enforce local codes and ordinances. And to be sure, violations of underage possession and consumption increased by 1,400 percent and 200 percent, respectively. Any local resident with a sense of pride would have been ashamed at the report of attendees urinating all over the side of the Costa Building—which housed the downtown police station—and producing a "literal river of urine" in its parking lot. More things proved to be black eyes on the event in the view of the police, but significantly, there were no deaths, massive injuries, riotous situations, or anything that would cause a stampede or other mob-rule activity.

Because, of course, they weren't charged with maintaining law and order, the fans were, for the most part, completely taken in by a sense of newfound friendship, kinship, and well-being. Stephen Dubberly, who came in from Tifton, Georgia, had a pretty standard take on things. "Free show [plus] broke college kids [equals] pandemonium," he said. "It was a free-for-all from my perspective. I was nineteen years old and felt like I was part of something huge for the first time in my life." Paul Eason, who had found that last-minute dump of a hotel room, said, "It was an absolute free-for-all, but in a cool way. You could do anything you wanted, and it was cool as long as you didn't hurt someone. We were close to the stage, and we saw a helicopter flying over with a camera filming the event. It was the biggest party in the country, and most people had no earthly idea, which is another reason it was cool. It was a feeling like we had found something cool, something sacred that 90 percent of people were clueless about. You looked at strangers and just smiled and nodded your head. It was like a collective conscious[ness] of people who just wanted to have fun!"

That helicopter and its low-light video-recording system belonged to the GBI. Its use, among other equipment and personnel, proved so expensive—$39,000 and change—that the agency told the ACC Police it would not be available for future events of this sort.

The overwhelming majority of the crowd was college-age or older. Some families brought the whole clan, and other families strictly forbade their kids from attending. That didn't stop teenaged Summer Self from pulling the old Sally Simpson and telling her parents that she was spending the night at a friend's house.[3] She had been specifically told not to go see Widespread Panic. As fate would have it, a family friend working security at the show busted her. And as fate unfolded further, the band's "Ain't Life Grand" was played later at her wedding, and she named each of her cats after Panic songs.

Claustrophobia was real, though, and for some it was unbearable. Who could blame them? "I just recall so many people crowding up front when there was absolutely no space to go. People were crawling up the gutter downspouts on the buildings to try and get a better view.

Only problem was, they were also falling off them too. It was a crazy, strange scene," said David Powell, who made the trip from Atlanta. "I withstood the first set but could not stand the packed crowd. I recall people not being able to move to go to the restroom, so they just did it right there in the street. I literally could not move left or right, so when I decided to head back to more open confines, I had to just go with the flow of the crowd to the side of the street and then worked my way back until there was enough room to break free. Luckily, I found my friend with no problem, which was a miracle in a crowd of a hundred thousand people and before the convenience of cell phones. Funny thing was, I don't remember the show itself being all that amazing, but it was the environment and the scene going on around it that made for such a great experience."

When conducting the research for this book, I encountered many gracious and generous people who shared their stories with me. Their universal assessment, to varying degrees of memory, was that this was a once-in-a-lifetime happening and that they couldn't be more thrilled to have had a part in it. Several of their stories were slated for inclusion here. Some had to be cut due to space considerations, and others I left out because, while supremely entertaining and undoubtedly special and personal, they contained much of the same sentiment and activity of the ones that have already been mentioned.

By show's end, the band couldn't believe they had pulled it off. They had done it. A wave of relief washed over them just as surely as actual rain began to fall during the last part of the final encore. "For us, that was so perfect because it [signaled the] end of the show, and everybody went inside, and they cleared the streets. It was just such a great feeling. I remember leaving the 40 Watt with Dave and Ellie and some other people and running into a policeman for the first time [that day]," said Mary Armstrong Dugas. Amazingly, the cops were all smiles. She asked them, "Hey, how was your night tonight? Is everything good?" She added, "I had a bit of a pit in my stomach waiting to hear that something bad had happened. But they all had big smiles on their faces and said, 'It was fantastic. People were great, people were polite. Everything went great.'"

"Everybody [dispersed] immediately after the show in a fairly calm way. But how do you disperse that many people that calmly? It was just like, 'Wow! That happened!' It basically felt like we got away with something," said John Bell. In actuality, and with no exaggeration, they had. For all the planning, Panic in the Streets was an event held in an area with no permanent and dedicated infrastructure. It was just a city street in a small town. "I think everybody learned a lot," said Dave Schools. "Towns like Athens just didn't do things like that, and if they did, they did them through the college. [This was] akin to Woodstock, in that they expected a certain amount of people and prepared for them, and then ten times as many showed up."

When the final costs to the city were tallied up the next month, they totaled $55,148.55. That amount didn't include, of course, Widespread Panic's expenses for staging, lighting, and electrical improvements. But it did mean that all city bills were paid in full and that Athens–Clarke County was made whole. None of this was obvious as the concert ended, though. The parting of the crowd into every nook and cranny in town revealed a sea of garbage and trash as far as the eye could see—and at least in the immediate concert vicinity, ankle deep.

"At the end of it—the worst part, if you ask me—was all the trash. There were places where it was two or three feet thick of trash covering the whole street. It's not that the attendees were slobs. It's just that there were so many people, they couldn't even get to a trash can," said Jared Bailey. "We were out there trying to pick it up by hand. I got there at six in the morning to meet the stage and do all that stuff, and then [at six] the next morning, and I'm walking round picking up trash . . . I couldn't walk anymore. That part to me was the worst part because it's just the aftermath and it's the end of it." Peter Jackson had seen his volunteers disappear into the mist of the night, and the Brown Cat crew was left to its own devices to ensure that all the band's equipment was safe, secure, and out of Mother Nature's way.

"[The volunteers were] just these very young, very sort of shell-shocked—I mean, bless their hearts—but very limited number of people. I mean, it was just like these were the kids who have now gone on to be, like, serious civil servants or something. You know, serious people who are now in the military or flying airplanes or are doctors or something. Not the bunch of fuckin' riffraff that follows around Widespread Panic," Jackson said. "This very sort of postapocalyptic air set down on Washington Street when the thing was over, because it was fuckin' trashed. And it got very dark and very quiet. The normal hustle and bustle of a rock show being loaded out by a bunch of professionals did not exist. It was like one excruciating piece at a time. So eventually, as daybreak was very close on the horizon, we sort of got it buttoned up to where it was like, 'OK, all the shit that can't get wet or stolen is at least in a truck locked up somewhere.'"

Immediately following the show, as the crowd dispersed to find parties or food, or to head back to their cars for sleep, Government Mule was readying to headline the after-show at the 40 Watt. In a very cheeky move, every ticket for the standing-room-only venue was printed with "Seat No. 420." The Waffle House at the corner of Alps Road and Broad Street ran out of waffle batter for the first time in its history. For a southerner, that is a completely unheard-of occurrence, akin to blasphemy and worthy of teeth gnashing. Every available beer in town seemed to have been emptied and its container thrown in the street. Cleanup efforts continued through the night, as promised, and Solid Waste Department trucks and street sweepers were eventually dispatched.

As day was breaking, Chuck Bertolina—still camped in the C&S parking lot with his wife and child—stepped outside his RV and looked around. Through the weekend he had been eyeing the four-foot-long banners celebrating the concert that were hung several feet high, and presumably out of reach, on downtown light poles. All but one had been torn from its roost during the night. "As I walked around, I met a gentlemen that I soon found out was a city official who, like me, wanted to see the scene the day after," he said. "We talked for about thirty minutes and got along very well. I mentioned that I really wanted one of the banners. He said they don't even belong to the band. The city made them, so they own them, [and] it would be theft if I took one. As we were about to part, he said, 'I'll tell you what. I'm gonna walk away and not look back. You go ahead and try to get one, but I don't think you will. They are attached with screws and bands.'" Bertolina looked around, scored a long pole from behind a building, managed to borrow a screwdriver from a Solid Waste truck driver, tied it all up with some plastic bags, and got to work. It took him half an hour of strain-inducing work, but his dedication unseated the banner from its four-screw footing. As it clanged to the ground, the noise reverberated around him to such a degree that he heard the "zip, zip, zip" of the surrounding tents opening. His fellow fans looked on in awe as he packed his fought-for treasure away and prepared to head home.

AIN'T LIFE GRAND
An Epilogue

So that's the story.

Most of the people involved in the direct planning of Panic in the Streets still think the event was a net positive for Athens even though it forced some growing pains on the city. In the ensuing twenty years large outdoor events—the most common being the annual AthFest— have become quite common on Washington Street. An entire generation of Athenians has grown up never knowing that they were once unheard of. Unintentionally, Panic in the Streets was a harbinger of change. The departments that once shoved a shoulder at such an idea are now streamlined and experienced to handle such things. Though there has never been another event in Athens like it, and may never be, at a minimum all involved got this one under their belt and can well handle anything that gets thrown their way. As Athens passed into the twenty-first century, those who had been in town for a while knew things were changing. Panic in the Streets was something of a catalyst that forced rapid change and adjustment. Its success is decidedly one of the reasons that not long afterward, marketing materials for Athens featuring bulldogs in sunglasses and chilling out with guitars appeared. Athens was now a music town as opposed to being simply a place with a killer music scene. As the first decades of the new century progressed, it would become much more difficult to find that oddball, inexpensive residence where a band could live together and hash out its material. More live venues opened, some closed, but nearly every bar in town now has a stage of some sort, and live music is a seven-night-a-week phenomenon.

Other things happened more incrementally but have been no less decisive. The real estate and retail landscape of downtown Athens is only about half as recognizable as it was in 1998. Gigantic high-rise condominiums and semi-luxury hotels dot the skyline. The Georgia Theatre is no longer a lovable jam-band dump with hippies everywhere; since a rebuilding effort after a devastating fire in 2009, it is a beautiful world-class facility that harks back to its days as a grand theatre with the latest feature attractions.

But bands do still find their way and hash it all out in rented houses. People still throw massive parties where young up-and-comers play their house-show best while crammed in a basement between a water heater and a washing machine. Every week some new group takes its first baby steps into the history of this scene and onto its own path. Somewhere out there is another Widespread Panic. Actually, they are all around, every day. But they don't look like ours or sound like ours and aren't necessarily remotely similar in style or audience. But they're young, hungry artists who have felt the urge, gotten the itch, and followed their spark.

When we turn around and take an inventory, the things that are different now seem obvious and, for some, acutely painful as nostalgia takes hold and wraps its roots around the fresh air of the day. But as noted in the first pages of this book: change happens. Its inevitability is as certain as the sun rising, and for those of us who love this town, no matter what happens, the sun always rises on Athens, Georgia. This book was never intended to be a biography of Widespread Panic (and it isn't!), nor any type of final treatise or history of the Athens music scene (and it isn't!). It's a story about a thing that happened in a very special place at a very special time with very special people. The thing's sheer size and long-lasting effects made it a ripe subject for a book. The history of Athens music is an ongoing conversation that is, largely, passed along orally from generation to generation. The ones with the best memories, though, are still the ones who thought to take a photograph or jot down some notes or salvage a favorite band's flyer from a downtown kiosk or nightclub wall. These moments in time—and they are mere moments—add up quickly, and soon these increments are sizably measurable and, occasionally, unbelievable. The only thing left to say is—no matter what scene you are in, or what town, or what situation—take a breath, look around, and remember where you are.

Because sometimes, even though we move ever forward, it can be nice to look back and remember the honest tunes and other things that have taken us this far.

NOTES

All direct quotations without source references in the main text or the end-notes are taken from interviews and e-mail correspondence conducted by the author from June to August 2017.

CHAPTER 1. Going Back

1. The actual title of the song is in dispute as being either "Going Back to Athens Town" or the more casual "Goin' Back." Although the latter certainly sounds more colloquially southern, the song is credited as the former on recordings made decades ago by the Dixie Redcoat Band.

2. *Red and Black*, December 4, 1969, 7.

3. *Red and Black*, November 10, 1971, 4.

4. Ibid., 1.

5. *People Magazine*, January 1983.

6. G. Loewenstein, T. O'Donoghue, and M. Rabin, "Projection Bias in Predicting Future Utility," *Quarterly Journal of Economics* 118, no. 4 (2003): 1209–48.

CHAPTER 2. This Part of Town

1. *Red and Black*, February 5, 1998, 1.

CHAPTER 3. Barstools and Dreamers

1. *Red and Black*, September 17, 1982, 8.

CHAPTER 4. Proving Ground

1. S. A. Reed, "Crowd Noise and the Hyperreal," paper presented at the Art of Record Production conference, University of Westminster, September 18, 2005, http://salexanderreed.com/crowd-noise-and-the-hyperreal, accessed August 28, 2017.

2. Ibid.

CHAPTER 5. Lawyers, Guns, and Money

1. "Woman Fights for Dream of Quiet April Wedding," *Augusta Chronicle*, March 18, 1998.

2. Perry Holt, "Georgia's City Governments," *New Georgia Encyclopedia*, June 6, 2017, www.georgiaencyclopedia.org/articles/counties-cities-neighborhoods/georgias-city-governments, accessed August 31, 2017.

3. "Mayor," Athens–Clarke County Unified Government website, https://www.athensclarkecounty.com/315/Mayor, accessed August 31, 2017.

CHAPTER 7. Travelin' Light Is the Only Way to Fly

1. *Red and Black*, April 17, 1998, 5.

CHAPTER 9. Raise the Roof

1. *Red and Black*, April 20, 1998, 3.

2. A right arrow (>) indicates that a song flows seamlessly into the next one; a comma indicates a break or pause between songs.

3. Simpson, a teenage character in the Who's rock opera *Tommy*, defies her parents and sneaks out to go see her favorite musician.

MUSIC OF THE AMERICAN SOUTH

Whisperin' Bill Anderson: An Unprecedented Life in Country Music
by Bill Anderson, with Peter Cooper

Party Out of Bounds: The B-52's, R.E.M., and the Kids
Who Rocked Athens, Georgia
by Rodger Lyle Brown

Widespread Panic in the Streets of Athens, Georgia
by Gordon Lamb